Praise for Something in the Water

"Michael W. Waters is not just a preacher--though he is emerging as one of the best--he's a leader, an organizer, professor, author and poet, and perhaps most importantly, a prophet. In *Something in the Water*, he reminds us that America's original sin of racism is insidious and ever-present, and must be boldly confronted and thoroughly dismantled if we are ever to move forward as a true multi-racial democracy. This is a compelling and transforming book that is coming out at exactly the right time, and I would especially urge all Christians to read it--and be inspired to both speak and act. As Dr. Waters reminds us, the arc of the moral universe only bends towards justice when we do the courageous work of that bending." —**Jim Wallis, founder of Sojourners and *New York Times* bestselling author of *Christ in Crisis***

"Michael Waters wades into the liminal space between the Civil Rights Movement and the current movements for racial justice in America and reminds us of just how far we have not come. Through his narratives, Waters shows how the personal is always political and the private easily becomes public for black and brown people from the sea-to-shining-sea of white supremacy in America. However, the current movements for racial justice afoot beckon us to jump in and get into 'good trouble' as a prophetic witness that *God's gonna trouble the water*." —**Leah Gunning Francis, Ph.D., Vice-President for Academic Affairs at Christian Theological Seminary and author of *Ferguson and Faith: Sparking Leadership and Awakening Community***

"The voice of Michael Waters booms from the pages of this book -- filled with personal narrative and poetry -- like a thunder-call for justice. Waters' work here captures the frustration, the grief, and yes, even the rage that comes with racial justice work. But it also captures something far more important: hope. Here in these pages, mixed in with the maddening stories of how whiteness will obstruct justice at every turn, Waters consistently points us back to a God who feels it all – a God who is with us in the resistance, a God whose heart bends toward justice. The perfect combination of historical journal, personal essay, and poetry, this book should be required reading for every American." —**Kerry Connelly, author, *Good* White Racist: Confronting***

D0819276

"In *Something in the Water*, Waters vividly recounts the ongoing and painful legacy of racism in America, a legacy that I bear in my body from a bomb detonated at Sixteenth Street Baptist Church in Birmingham in 1963 which took the life of my sister, Addie Mae, the lives of our three friends, and rendered me partially blind. As I continue to seek justice for the pain and suffering that I have endured, I am grateful to know that through Waters' words, my journey has not been forgotten, and through Waters' work, the moral arc is still being bent towards justice." —**Sarah Collins Rudolph, author of *The 5th Little Girl: Soul Survivor of the 16th Street Baptist Church Bombing (The Sarah Collins Rudolph Story)***

"Every white Christian like me needs a black pastor and teacher. In Rev. Dr. Michael Waters, I also get a prophet as well. I love and respect this man so much, and I am grateful that this rich collection of insightful writings is available so that more and more of us can be among his congregation -- not just to be instructed in mind and inspired in spirit, but also to be motivated for action in our ongoing movement toward a more perfect union and beloved community." —**Brian D. McLaren, author and activist**

"The Reverend Dr. Michael Waters is a faith leader with a deep moral conscience who inspires with his words and actions daily. Having been by his side through many moments of struggle, it is a blessing he lets us into his thoughts that keep him going, and keep us thinking." —**Imam Dr. Omar Suleiman, professor, and founder/president of the Yaqeen Institute for Islamic Research**

"*Something in the Water* is a must-read. A refreshing narrative about what we continue to face in America with a new fresh context and raw truth telling, by one of today's most esteemed scholars, a young and woke pastor, teacher, husband, and father in today's political and religious arenas."–**Sharon Risher, activist and author, *For Such a Time as This: Hope and Forgiveness after the Charleston Massacre***

"Michael Waters is a powerful voice for change in America. His words will grip you from the very first page and not let you go until you are convicted to fight for racial justice, whoever you are, wherever you are." —**Doug Pagitt, author, pastor, social activist, and executive director of Vote Common Good.**

Something in the Water

A 21ˢᵗ Century Civil Rights Odyssey

Michael W. Waters

Foreword by Beto O'Rourke

**chalice
press**

Saint Louis, Missouri

Copyright ©2020 by Chalice Press

Bible quotations, unless otherwise noted, are from the *New Revised Standard Version Bible*, copyright 1989, Division of Christian Education of the National Council of the Churches of Christ in the United States of America. Used by permission. All rights reserved.

ChalicePress.com

Print: 9780827235496
EPUB: 9780827235502
EPDF: 9780827235519

Printed in the United States of America

For the Martyrs and the Ancestors

And with Kingian hope that my own children will one day live in
a nation where they will not be judged by the color of their skin,
but by the content of their character.

Till justice flows like waters, and righteousness
like a mighty stream ...

Table of Contents

Foreword

Themes flow together to produce ideas, much like tributaries converge to form rivers, in Michael Waters' latest book, *Something in the Water: A 21st Century Civil Rights Odyssey*. The poems, speeches, reflections, and essays read together like the "mighty stream" he often invokes at the end of a eulogy or sermon.

One of the powerful ideas that Waters surges to the surface is that progress isn't inevitable. In raising Dr. Martin Luther King Jr.'s oft-quoted line about the arc of the moral universe bending toward justice, Waters reminds us that it bends only when we have the courage to bend it. And when the courage leaves us, when complacency sets in, when we sleep through the revolution and the oppressor rides free of accountability, not only do we stop moving forward, we lose ground and give up much of what so many before us fought and died to gain.

It helps to explain how there are fewer Black homeowners today than in 1968, the year of Dr. King's murder.

How incarceration rates—driven by a war on drugs that is really a war on people, and especially people of color—have increased by 700 percent.

How our public schools are today more segregated in many communities than at any time since 1954.

And how there is now ten times more wealth in white America than there is in Black America.

Through anecdote and data, story and facts, as well as his own lived experiences, Waters gives the lie to the idea that Dr. King believed in the inevitability of justice—an idea that often is invoked to comfort the powerful as well as the powerless. This twisting of King's intent has allowed some to preach a promise that without work or sacrifice we somehow will arrive at justice; and, when swallowed whole, that promise lulls us into self-defeating complacency and complicity.

No, Dr. King certainly didn't believe that. As Waters reminds us, he was the man who shared this truth in "Letter from Birmingham Jail," that "freedom is never given voluntarily by the oppressor; it must be demanded by the oppressed."

Rev. Waters, this man of faith, brings us to the conclusion that it's not enough to simply believe. "Faith without works is dead," he reminds us as he shares the story of Botham Jean's family, here in the United States to recover his body and seek justice for his murder at the hands of a white police officer. After a meditation on the stunning act of grace and mercy shown by Botham's brother at the officer's sentencing, Waters brings in Jean's mother, who updates James's first-century letter in her own words. "I want to see change," she says. "Talk but no action means nothing."

If America is indeed stuck, as Waters contends, between its foundational promise and the realization of that promise; between progress and reaction; between hope and resignation, then the answer must be action.

That's where his flow of ideas and stories, martyrs and heroes, and family members and perfect strangers delivers the reader. Action is the antidote to despair, the answer to our prayers, and the key to victory.

So, we must move, take action, and put our faith in motion. "Lord," Waters implores, "teach me to pray with my feet."

Beto O'Rourke
El Paso, Texas

2

Introduction

On Saturday, August 3, 2019, I was sitting quietly in my office amid a buzz of activity across our church campus. Our church was preparing to burn our mortgage the following day. Our youth were rehearsing their dance performance for the service. We were eagerly anticipating the arrival of our bishop and other special invited guests to help us celebrate this important milestone, and, as their pastor, I was beaming with excitement and anticipation. I leaned back in my chair and picked up my phone to peruse social media.

There was a breaking news alert notification.
There had been another mass shooting.
This time it was in El Paso.
My heart sank.

Over the next hours and days, we learned that a young white supremacist and domestic terrorist had driven some six hundred and fifty miles from Allen, Texas, just north of Dallas, to unleash hell upon unsuspecting back-to-school shoppers at an El Paso Walmart superstore. When the melee was over, forty-six people were shot and twenty-two were dead. The twenty-third person died after several months in the hospital.

El Paso, Texas, is an American border city, the nation's twenty-second largest with almost seven hundred thousand residents. It sits along the Rio Grande across the Mexico-United States border from Cuidad Juarez (the City of Juarez), a metropolis of 1.4 million residents.

El Paso is a beloved American city with a unique history, culture, and composition. The Sun Bowl played annually in El Paso is the second-oldest NCAA football bowl game in America. In 1966, the Texas Western College of the University of Texas (now University of Texas at El Paso) men's basketball team became the first to start five Black players in a championship game as they defeated the University of Kentucky for the national championship. El Paso is home to Fort Bliss, one of the largest army military bases in America, and was named America's safest city twice in the 2010s. Over 80 percent of El Paso's residents are Latinx, the highest percentage for any American city.

For me, El Paso is the repository of some of my happiest and most formative childhood memories. As a youth, I made annual odysseys to El Paso to spend a portion of my summer vacation with my paternal grandparents, Ollie and Marie Waters. I learned to swim at the local YMCA in El Paso.

My grandmother possessed only a third-grade education because her labor often was needed to help the family bring in the East Texas harvest. She was a consummate chef who seemed to live her days in the kitchen, pulling a steady stream of delectables off her stove and out of her oven. Pancakes, eggs, and bacon for breakfast; fried chicken, mashed potatoes, and green beans for lunch (yes, lunch); and what felt like a Thanksgiving meal each night for dinner. She cooked each day as though she was still cooking for her family of six. She even found time to bake fresh gingerbread and cookies.

I did not mind any of this.

My grandfather, an expert mechanic who worked for years on the base, was a jolly character. I would curl up in bed with him every Sunday night to read the Sunday morning paper "funnies." One of my great joys was riding along with him across El Paso to visit friends and run errands. My grandparents have long since departed, but the memory of their compassion and generosity remains with me.

My fond and loving memories of El Paso were invaded that Saturday morning by the murderous impulse of this young terrorist. Before carrying out his heinous deed, he had posted a manifesto on the Internet about protecting the state from the so-called "Hispanic invasion," words he'd heard uttered by the forty-fifth president of the United States.

The El Paso shooter is not the only terrorist who has been motivated to act on the forty-fifth president's rhetoric, so the attack there should have been anticipated. Researchers already had noted a dramatic increase in racially motivated violence in the regions where President Donald Trump had held a rally. It could have happened in any American city, but this time it hit close to home for me.

It's amazing how strangers find their lives colliding at the axis of tragedy. The victims' stories are gripping in that each of them was engaged in routine activity. Nothing seemed especially different about the day. It was just another Saturday to pick up a few items at Walmart.

Andre and Jordan Anchondo had gone shopping with their two-month-old son, Paul, after dropping off their six-year-old daughter at cheerleading practice. Andre, just twenty-three years old, jumped in front of the terrorist to shield his wife, Jordan, twenty-five, who shielded their baby with her body. When their bodies were recovered, Andre's body was covering Jordan, and she was covering her infant's tiny body. The baby's clothing was soaked in his parents' blood. He'd suffered broken fingers, but neither parent survived.

Margie Reckard, sixty-three, had gone to the Walmart superstore to do grocery shopping, leaving her husband, Antonio Basco, at home to do maintenance on their SUV. For several hours after the massacre, Basco drove to hospitals across the region searching for his wife. He ultimately received the heartbreaking news that she was among the dead.

The shooting victims ranged in age from two to eighty. Those who didn't survive were as young as age fifteen and as old as ninety. They were Americans, Mexicans, and one German. All created in the image of God.

May God bless the dead.

* * * * *

I did not watch the news coverage as it aired live on the scene, but the week following the massacre, I was perusing social media when I stumbled upon an MSNBC video segment featuring commentator and Princeton University professor Eddie Glaude. I knew of Dr. Glaude's work and recently had made his controversial 2013 *Huffington Post* article, "The Black Church Is Dead," required reading for the Ministry in the Black Church course I had taught at the SMU Perkins School of Theology, my alma mater, earlier that summer. During the segment, Dr. Glaude masterfully, passionately, and even poetically expanded the narrative of racial violence in America well beyond El Paso and the era of Donald Trump:

> America's not unique in its sins. As a country, we're not unique in our evils. I think where we may be singular is our refusal to acknowledge them. And the legends and myths we tell about our inherent goodness, to hide and cover and conceal so that we can maintain a kind of willful ignorance that protects our innocence.

Dr. Glaude continued,

> It's easy for us to place it all on Donald Trump's shoulders. It's easy for us to place Pittsburgh on his shoulders. It's easy for me to place Charlottesville on his shoulders. It's easy for us to place El Paso on his shoulders. *This is us.* And if we're going to get past this, we can't blame it on him.

He went on,

> He's a manifestation of the ugliness that's in us. Either we're going to change ... or we're going to do

this again and again, and babies are going to have to grow up without mothers and fathers, uncles and aunts, friends, while we're trying to convince white folk to finally leave behind a history that will maybe, maybe—or embrace a history that might set them free from being white. Finally.

Dr. Glaude's words had gone viral. As they did with many people across America, his words resonated with me. The ugliness being perpetuated across America was much bigger than Donald Trump, its roots far deeper.

Although it is without debate that Donald Trump both inspired and gave cover to acts of hate and racial violence, Trump was at best a by-product of this American ugliness—a symptom but not the source. As Dr. Glaude pointed out, "This is us!" And as rapper Childish Gambino had announced in song over a year prior, "This is America!"

White supremacy comes with a body count, and the bodies bear witness against our national mythology. Violence and hate are not apart from us. It has always been closer to our core as Americans than we have cared to acknowledge. There is something troubled, even tainted, in the waters of America that we must explore, and until our nation fully has a reckoning with these realities, we will revisit these atrocities and brutalities in each generation.

* * * * *

In truth, my travels throughout 2019, both before and after the El Paso massacre, had confirmed for me that there is something in the water of America with which we must fully contend. I began the year on the West Coast near the calm waters of the Pacific Ocean, preaching and lecturing near and around the Los Angeles area at various Dr. Martin Luther King Jr. holiday commemorations on the ninetieth anniversary of his birth.

After preaching in South Central the Sunday morning before the holiday, we left the church and headed to Watts Towers in the city of Watts. A half century ago, Watts had been ablaze—the result of an uprising among young Black Americans after yet another act of police brutality against a brother in the community. Amid these uprisings, Dr. King had traveled to the area to promote a nonviolent direct action response to the horrors that Los Angeles' Black community had faced. His efforts failed; there was nothing he could do to quell the fires that burned without and within.

During an interview on September 27, 1966, with *CBS News*'s Mike Wallace, Dr. King offered a stunning articulation of the meaning of violent protests and uprisings. Wallace questioned Dr. King concerning the "increasingly vocal minority" who, like the young people of Watts, disagreed with his calls for nonviolence.

Dr. King responded, "I contend that the cry of 'Black power' is, at bottom, a reaction to the reluctance of white power to make the kind of changes necessary to make justice a reality for the Negro. I think that we've got to see that a riot is the language of the unheard. And what is it that America has failed to hear? It has failed to hear that the economic plight of the Negro poor has worsened over the last few years."

Following our visit to the Watts Towers, we journeyed south to have dinner in Long Beach, a city perched on the beautiful blue ocean water. The picturesque view of this city was yet another reminder that a pollutant in our waters has infected a people. *Pacific* is derived from the Latin word associated with peace; yet beneath this seemingly placid blue water is a long and disturbing history overflowing with acts of racism and injustice that have extended beyond people with Black and Brown skin.

In 1942, two months after the Japanese attack on Pearl Harbor, President Franklin Delano Roosevelt signed Executive Order 9066, authorizing the relocation of all people deemed a threat to national security from the West Coast to internment camps farther inland. Japanese Americans, like Jews in Europe during the Third Reich, were systematically corralled to containment facilities like criminals. These camps operated on American soil for as many as four years, holding innocent American citizens behind barbed wire-fenced encampments without the right to due process. The US government eventually disbursed more than $1.6 billion in reparations to 82,219 Japanese Americans who had been interned. Although reparations are at least an acknowledgement that harm was done, the racist, xenophobic hatred toward Americans that produced these camps resulted in losses that cannot be measured in dollars alone. Financial compensation cannot account for the loss of livelihood, loss of trust, and loss of dignity—crimes against humanity for which no one was ever convicted.

These crimes of injustice run deep in the tumultuous waters of American history.

Since 2005, I have led groups to visit cities and sites that are significant to the American civil rights movement to meet and dialogue with persons—some well-known, others not—who made invaluable contributions to the cause of justice. In February 2019, I led such a pilgrimage through the Deep South. Our first stop was in Glendora, Mississippi. Guided by the city's mayor, Johnny B. Thomas, we visited the place where fourteen-year-old Emmett Till's mutilated body was pulled from the water.

I was struck by the fact that these waters were adjacent to the rich soil of plantation grounds where generations of Black workers toiled in the hot Mississippi sun to harvest cotton. Between the water's edge and the road that ran past the old plantation grounds stood a memorial marker commemorating young Till. And just like Till, the sign has been ravaged repeatedly, riddled with bullets, and discarded into the water as rubbish; so many times, in fact, that an updated sign was made from bulletproof material. Our visit, however, came before the sign had been replaced, and we bore witness to the bullet holes that were present in the defaced sign. The entire experience caused me to ponder how racial hated could be so intense and so pervasive that later generations desired to harm the very memory of this child who lost his life for a deed that his accuser later admitted was a lie.

I grabbed some remnants from the cotton field that already had been harvested. For the remainder of the day, I pondered Mayor Thomas' words, who explained that what had happened to Emmett Till was not out of the ordinary. The people who lived there during that era accepted that "they were always pulling up Black bodies from these waters," as the mayor explained rather matter-of-factly.

In April, I made two visits to Virginia, home of the first permanent European settlement that ultimately led to the establishment of the United States of America. The first visit was to accompany my wife as she gave a presentation at a conference in Charlottesville. While there, we paid our respects at a narrow pass where Heather Heyer—a young white woman killed by a white supremacist while giving public witness and service to the mattering of Black lives—became the Viola Liuzzo of her generation. We also paused to gaze upon the Confederate monument that had drawn young white supremacists there from across the nation in August 2017. Their mission was to terrorize the city as they marched through Charlottesville streets into the night, wielding torches and chanting, "You will not replace us!" Their mantra was extracted from a white supremacist conspiracy theory called "the Great Replacement," which also was present in the El Paso terrorist's manifesto.

In between my visits to Virginia, I led another civil rights pilgrimage in April. We crossed the Alabama River, a major water thoroughfare for transporting the kidnapped Africans who had been forced into slavery. In Montgomery, we visited the stunning National Memorial for Peace and Justice, referred to by some as the "National Lynching Memorial," and the EJI Legacy Museum, which had served as a holding pen where enslaved Blacks sat in bonds as they waited to be sold on the auction block. The city of Montgomery, the first capital of the Confederate States of America and seat of its national government, was one of the most prominent domestic slave trading posts in America. Commerce Street—which today runs directly behind the Legacy Museum and makes a direct line between the Alabama River and the main slave auction site—was the route where Black human captives were paraded in chains.

I returned to Virginia a few weeks later to speak for internationally renowned music producer/artist Pharrell Williams' inaugural Something in the Water Festival in Virginia Beach. One of his executives had heard me speak in Los Angeles earlier in the year, so I was invited to bring a message during Sunday's pop-up church service on the beach. The crowd of more than five thousand participants was impressive, but I was more awed by the location where I was standing than by the size of the audience to whom I was speaking. I was struck by the massive sight of primarily Black bodies situated upon the very shores of the Atlantic Ocean where my kidnapped forebears had entered forced bondage four hundred years prior. I was standing less than an hour from the location where they docked.

As I looked out upon a sea of people, then upon the sea of water, I saw more than an ocean. I saw a watery mass grave. From my study of history, in the moment I was painfully aware that the slave insurance purchased by slave traffickers did not cover infirmed bodies brought ashore who were too sick to work. Only bodies that died while in transit were eligible for a claim. Therefore, sick Africans often were thrown overboard to drown so that the traffickers could collect their insurance money. On at least one noted occasion, white locals complained against this practice, not because of the sheer disregard for human life, but rather because those bodies later washed ashore, bringing a great stench from their decomposition.

In June, as my wife attended a Columbia University conference on criminal justice reform, I sat in MSNBC's New York studio with the Reverend Sharon Risher. The winter prior, I was honored to write the foreword to Rev. Risher's book, *For Such a Time as This: Hope and Forgiveness after the Charleston*

Massacre. On June 17, 2015, Rev. Risher's mother, Ethel Lance, and eight others were murdered by a young white supremacist domestic terrorist at the close of the Wednesday night Bible study at Emanuel AME Church. A month after the tragedy, I traveled to Charleston, where I personally bore witness to bullet holes in the church—bullets that missed or went through the bodies of church members and lodged in the walls and floors.

Her book had been featured on *The Today Show* earlier that morning, and we were in the greenroom of MSNBC's studio, where she was waiting to discuss the book with Craig Melvin. Interestingly, I had been interviewed by Mr. Melvin three summers prior in Dallas after five police officers were killed by an assailant after a peaceful protest and march that bore witness to the brutal police killings of Alton Sterling in New Orleans and Philando Castile near Minneapolis.

In one of the most gripping portions of her book, Rev. Risher wrote, "As Americans and as citizens of the country, we continue to address racism and gun violence only cosmetically." In her foreword, I wrote, "It is painful to note that we can mark time in America by who has been shot and when."

As we visited there on Manhattan Island, surrounded by the waters of the East River, the Hudson River, the Harlem River, and the Atlantic Ocean, I reflected on Seneca Village, the nineteenth-century settlement of Black landowners—the first of its kind in the city of New York. Established in 1825 by free Blacks, Seneca Village once boasted 264 residents, three churches, a school, and two cemeteries. In 1857, New York claimed the land by eminent domain, tore down the homes, and created Central Park. I could not help but link the harms done to this Black community in 1857 to the harms done when five Black teenagers were falsely accused of assaulting a white woman in Central Park, wherein they conceded to confessions coerced by the police. These five young men collectively served forty years in prison for a crime they did not commit. On May 1, 1989, Donald Trump, at the time earning millions as a New York real estate magnate, took out a full-page ad in the city's four major newspapers calling for a return of the death penalty. In the ad, for which he paid $85,000 in 1989, Trump wrote that he wanted the "criminals of every age" accused of harming the woman "to be afraid." Trump also wrote,

> Mayor Koch has stated that hate and rancor should be removed from our hearts. I do not think so. I want to hate these muggers and murderers. They should be forced to suffer ... Yes, Mayor Koch, I want to hate these murderers and I always will ... How can our great society tolerate the continued brutalization of its citizens by crazed misfits? Criminals must be told that their *civil liberties end when an attack on our safety begins!*

In August, I had the honor to speak at Broadmoor United Methodist Church in Baton Rouge, Louisiana. They had joined several other congregations across America in a church-wide study of my book, *Stakes Is High: Race, Faith, and Hope for America*, which won a National Wilbur Award in nonfiction. Unbeknownst to many, Baton Rouge was the site of the first successful bus boycott, and the Montgomery Bus Boycott was modeled after it. The late Dr. Gardner C. Taylor, regarded by many as the dean of Black preachers in America and a mentor of Dr. Martin Luther King Jr., was a prominent pastor and leader in the movement during the time of the boycott in Baton Rouge.

The day I arrived in Baton Rouge, officials had just announced that a settlement had been reached with Blane Salamoni, the former police officer who shot and killed Alton Sterling. In the terms of the settlement, Salamoni could resign from the department instead of being fired. Previously, state and federal officers had declined to prosecute Salamoni for Sterling's death, which had only intensified the tensions in the community. Amid this tension, the day before I arrived, another Black man had been killed by police. I was scheduled to meet with the 100 Black Men chapter of Baton Rouge, but they had to cancel to respond to the latest tragedy. It was not lost on me that yet another tragedy had interrupted a scheduled opportunity to faithfully engage a prior one.

My Baton Rouge hotel was situated was on the Mississippi River, where Black bodies once had been transported up and down that waterway for trade. At one point in history, a successful swim to the west bank of the Mississippi River could render an enslaved Black person free. I could not help but wonder how many of the enslaved had safely escaped to freedom and how many met their demise in the attempt.

In September, a month after the Walmart massacre, I made the familiar journey to El Paso. This time, I was there with Vote Common Good to observe a field hearing of the United States House Judiciary Committee's Subcommittee on Immigration and Citizenship, held on the University of Texas at El Paso campus. The "Oversight of the Trump Administration's Border Policies and the Relationship Between Anti-Immigrant Rhetoric and Domestic Terrorism" hearing, led by El Paso Congresswoman Veronica Escobar, focused on "conditions along the southern border and the violence aimed at the immigrant communities." While there, I had an opportunity to speak with Congresspersons Escobar, Sheila Jackson Lee (whom I had first met as a youth growing up in Houston), and Chairman Jerry Nadler.

I vividly remember the gripping witness testimony of Dr. Monica Muñoz Martinez, the Stanley J. Bernstein assistant professor of American Studies and Ethnic Studies at Brown University. Dr. Martinez powerfully noted that in Texas history, there is a tripartite intersection of atrocities that continues to shape politics in the state—the enslavement of Black bodies, the genocide of Indigenous nations, and the horrors of colonialism. She also noted that so many Mexican Americans were killed in Texas during the 1910s that the entire period is known as "The Massacre."

Following the Congressional hearing, we visited a safe house for refugees, then participated in a protest outside a detention center. I was invited to pray and to offer a benediction for the protest, and I even took a short interview with a local news station.

Following the protest, we made our way to that fateful Walmart, which had been transformed into a memorial for the fallen. Crosses, flowers, stuffed animals, candles, notes, artwork, and other signs of remembrance stretched across the expanse of fencing behind the temporarily closed superstore. I walked the full length of the memorial, attempting to take in each part.

As I reached the end of the memorial, I saw an elderly man carefully tending to the flowers situated around one of the crosses erected to honor the fallen. I did not want to disturb his work, but I recognized him from the news reports. It was Antonio Basco, Margie Reckard's widower. He had gained notoriety after he expressed concern that no one would be present to help him to mourn his wife's passing. His concern went viral, and masses of people showed up on the day of Margie's funeral in support of Antonio. So many came to share in his grief that they filled the church to capacity and formed a line that wrapped around the entire city block.

I approached Mr. Basco to let him know that he was not forgotten and that I was praying for him. He jumped to his feet, buried his head in my chest, and began to weep. Muffled under the sobs I heard, "I feel so alone." I attempted to pray words of comfort, then asked if we could take a photo together that I might share with others to request their prayers also. He readily agreed, and once posted, the picture went viral, along with prayers pouring in from all over the world. Later that evening, I spoke at a vigil and rally at the memorial before departing for Omaha, Nebraska the next day. I was scheduled to speak there over several days leading to the one hundredth anniversary of the Red Summer lynching of Will Brown, a Black man who had been murdered in front of the Douglas County Courthouse in downtown Omaha. He had been accused of raping a white woman but had had no opportunity to prove his innocence. Before a trial could occur, a white mob showed up at the courthouse demanding that Brown be handed over to them. Once released to the angry mob, Brown was hanged from a lamppost, riddled with bullets, and then tied and dragged behind a car before he was burned at the stake.

At the end of September, I traveled to Toronto to speak at a fundraising gala alongside my friend and brother, Imam Dr. Omar Suleiman, in support of Indigenous communities experiencing water crises. Canada, often celebrated as a liberal and tolerant nation, has a multitude of Indigenous communities who are without clean drinking water, some of whom must drive up to three hours one way to access clean water each week. Looking at their situation, I could not help but think of the people of Flint, Michigan—an overwhelmingly Black American city—who are still without clean drinking water.

In October, I was in Philadelphia to preach and to participate on a panel at Mother Bethel African Methodist Episcopal Church, the mother church of the AME denomination, and the birthplace of the Black liberation struggle in America. I traveled there to preach following the conviction of former Dallas police officer Amber Guyger, who had killed Botham Shem Jean in his own living room. I also spoke on a panel regarding Black forgiveness after experiencing racial violence alongside a Temple University professor and the daughter of another victim of the Mother Emanuel massacre.

Just prior the trip, my church had hosted the Jean family and other activists for a final press conference before they departed to their native Saint Lucia following the trial. As Botham's mother spoke before the reporters and cameras, she said, "I want to see change. Talk but no action means nothing." Mrs. Allison Jean's remarks were echoes of James 2:20: "Faith without works is dead."

We gathered just one mile east of the Trinity River, which for years had been polluted by the Columbia Packing Company, which threw pig blood and other animal remains into the water.

The contaminated water created a stench that penetrated the most densely populated Black communities of Dallas. The Caddo people that first called North Texas home named the river the Arkikosa. In a horror story repeated across America, an army led by General Edward Tarrant in 1841 massacred the Caddo people along the banks of the Arkikosa and burned down their homes—forgotten history for most North Texas. Later that same year, the white settlement that would become Dallas was established.

Blood has long flowed in the river.

I was grateful to travel to Philadelphia with my family. While there, we visited sites related to independence and to the founding of America. We took a bus tour of the city as well. As the bus tour was coming to an end, we passed the Delaware River and turned on Market Street. From my studies, I knew that a city's Market Street was likely the place where goods were sold. Also, given this nation's history, it was likely the place where Black captives were sold. As expected, right at the corner of the street—the last building before reaching the river—was a structure that housed Black bodies in preparation to sell them into enslavement.

We visited the Liberty Bell, displayed on the same grounds as the temporary residence of President George Washington. We learned that the enslaved worked at this temporary residence. To get around the Gradual Abolition Act of 1780—a Pennsylvania law that required the Black enslaved to be freed after their twenty-eighth birthday or after they had been moved from out of state to live and work there for six months—Washington, a founding father of America, routinely sent his enslaved out of state before their eligibility for emancipation so that he could reset the calendar and keep them in bondage. Ironically, farther down on Market Street, where Black bodies were held and later sold as slaves, the Declaration of Independence—which declares, "We hold these truths to be self-evident, that all men are created equal, that they are endowed by their Creator with certain unalienable Rights, that among these are Life, Liberty and the pursuit of Happiness"—was written. The hypocrisy of it all was almost more than I could bear.

Later that same week in October, I was invited to speak in Grand Prairie, Texas, a suburb of Dallas, as Beto O'Rourke, the charismatic former US Congressman from El Paso who had mounted a US presidential campaign, held a rally against fear, a counter-rally to President Trump's own rally being held simultaneously in downtown Dallas. It was again not lost on me that racial violence frequently followed Trump rallies in the regions in which they were held, and I was honored to stand in direct witness against the hatred that Trump was sure to spew. I not only addressed the capacity crowd, but I had the privilege of formally introducing Mr. Rourke that night as well. Amid what had been a harrowing year, it was a hopeful night, and I was grateful to be there and to be reminded of what America could become if we claimed the courage to stand together against marginalization, oppression, suppression, and injustices of all shapes and forms.

Fast forward to January 2020, which found me in Des Moines, Iowa, just ahead of the Iowa primaries. This was my first trip to the Hawkeye State, and it had special meaning for me. My late maternal grandfather, Bishop W. Williams, still the greatest man I have ever known, integrated the graduate program in biology at Iowa State University. While there, I had the privilege of once again hearing the exceptional Genesis Be, a Mississippi-born Black poet and rapper, as she delivered an original piece. The premise of her performance was this: What would happen in America if Donald Trump were to disappear? Would mass incarceration cease? Would racism, xenophobia, and hatred end? Would poverty be eradicated over night?

A couple of months before Donald Trump took office in early 2017, Dr. Johnathan Granoff, president of the Global Security Institute, wrote in a *Time Magazine* article that the forty-fifth president was an existential threat to the world.

Unfortunately, throughout his presidency, Trump has proven the accuracy of this statement. Still, as Dr. Glaude was so careful to communicate, America's ills run far deeper than Trump. These issues did not emerge with him, nor will they automatically end with him. No, as Glaude shared, *this is us*, and my recent travels had only affirmed this. From the Pacific to the Atlantic, from the Rio Grande to the Mighty Mississippi, from the Hudson to the Delaware, from the polluted waters of the Trinity River in Dallas to the undrinkable waters of the Flint River in Flint to the Tallahatchie River from which Emmett Till was dredged, and the many more that history has forgotten—there is something in the waters of America, literally and figuratively, that must be purified.

Let us call it toxic. Let us call it hate. Let us call it denying the humanity of all God's creation. Let us call it forsaking the image of God present in every human countenance. Let us call it evil. From the theft of Native lands to the lynching of Black and Brown bodies, from the burning down of the Greenwood District of Tulsa to the redlining of American cities that continues to define communities of racialized poverty today—*this is us*.

Our collective struggle and question yet unanswered is: Does this *still* have to be us? And if not, what are we willing to do to create a reality much better than what we possess now?

* * * * *

Over the past several years, I have crisscrossed America engaging diverse communities about racism's import into the twenty-first century. W. E. B. Du Bois declared in his seminal work, *The Souls of Black Folk*, "The problem of the twentieth century is the problem of the colorline."[1] I contend that this problem continues to define us today. Some have sought to dismiss this claim, offering instead that the primary problem we face is that of economic and wealth disparity, which has never been greater in our nation. Economics in America has always been racialized, and when you look at who remains at the bottom rung of America's economic ladder, we see what we have always seen—a sea of Black faces looking back.

When I speak in a new community, I often request to see the community's redlining map. Knowing little about the geography or social landscape of the city, I will place the map on a screen. Then I share with the crowd my prognosis that the redlined areas are either those places in the city that continue to experience the highest levels of poverty or they are the places that are experiencing the most rapid signs of gentrification. From Seattle to Charlotte, and many places in between, my speculation has yet to be proven wrong. Of redlined communities, 75 percent remain impoverished in America today, whereas 91 percent of the greenlined or "best" communities remain middle to upper-class and are 85-percent White. This national congruence of harm only solidifies that something problematic continues to endure in our nation's waters.

I have accepted the uniqueness of my odyssey into areas of the country greatly impacted by racism and xenophobia and the responsibility that inherently comes with it. As the gospels declare, and as my family frequently would share when I was a child, "to whom much is given, much is required."[2] I have been given the rare opportunity to bear witness to America's continuing struggle with racial injustice and racial inequity. Recognizing this fact, I have attempted to remain faithful to the requirements of my calling—whether speaking truth to power in the chambers of the United States House of Representatives or the Dallas City Hall, whether standing with family members who have lost loved ones to police brutality, or standing beside heroes of the American civil rights movement, or addressing thousands gathered in a stadium or thousands at a rally.

This volume contains some of my public reflections given as a part of my odyssey, categorized into three sections: Poems and Petitions; Laments and Public Liturgies; and Prophetic Proclamations. From poems and prayers to sermons and eulogies, from rally cries to commentaries, it illuminates not just our present struggles, but also my hope and belief in a better day to come. Some of these words were written immediately and with a sense of urgency given the happenings of the day. Others were written after private meditation, contemplation, and study. All were written with the hope of inspiring change.

As the late Tupac Amaru Shakur said,

> I'm not saying I'm gonna rule the world or I'm gonna change the world, but I guarantee you that I will spark the brain that will change the world. And that's our job, it's to spark somebody else watching us. We might not be the ones, but let's not be selfish and because we not gonna change the world let's not talk about how we should change it. I don't know how to change it, but I know if I keep talking about how dirty it is out here, somebody's gonna clean it up.[3]

I may not be as bold as Mr. Shakur to make such a guarantee, but I do pray that the words herein spark brains and inspire change.

The waters that define the social, political, theological, and economic landscapes of our nation are contaminated with the pollution of racism. It is dirty out here. If anyone is to clean it up, it must be us. If not for us, then for those who shall follow behind.

In Homer's ancient Greek epic poem *The Odyssey*, we find this striking observation: "Men are so quick to blame the gods: they say that we devise their misery. But they themselves—in their own depravity—design grief greater than the griefs that fate assigns." There is something in the waters of America that continually brings harm to Black, Brown, and Indigenous people. It is not there by accident, but rather by design. The grief it has wrought is immeasurable.

We must work to purify these waters until "justice flows like waters, and righteousness, like a mighty stream."

Something in the Water

POEMS AND PETITIONS

God Grieves: Contemplations amid Tragedy

While praying for the shooting victims in Orlando,
I remembered the souls still seeking clean water in Flint.

While remembering the residents of Flint,
I remembered the souls of kidnapped Africans drowned
in the Mediterranean Sea.

While remembering precious victims of
a tragic and watery demise,
I remembered still-grieving souls forced to mop the blood of
their beloved deceased members from the church's floor.

While remembering grieving souls in Charleston,
I remembered the weary soul of a homeless man seen
defecating in an open field.

While remembering this homeless man with his weary soul,
I remembered yet another young soul who took the life of
yet another young soul in my city.

While remembering lost young souls, I, too, remembered
battered souls, the souls of women and children, terrorized
daily at the hands of men who should love and protect them.

Then I remembered that God knows, feels, grieves, and is
present to witness all pain and suffering in our world.

I concluded that no one suffers more than God.

Then I said, "Amen."

A Prayer for Holy Soles

(Delivered January 9, 2019, in Dallas, Texas, during the Martin Luther King Jr. wreath-laying ceremony at Dallas City Hall just prior to the Dallas Black Clergy Agenda's nonviolent direct action protest and issuance of demands to Dallas City Council.)

Dear God,
    teach me to pray
    with my feet.

    The steps of the ancestors were sturdy and strong.
    They somehow carried them to cut down strange fruit
    dangling in the breeze.
    Up and down Montgomery's hills,
    To mass meetings, lunch counters, and courthouses
    To face canines, tear gas, and water hoses
    As bullets and bombs wrought martyrs,
    Their blood still crying out from the deep.

    LORD God,
    teach me to pray
    with my feet.

For those felled while adorned with hoodie, for those who still
can't breathe, for those whose hearts have been broken under
the weight of fathers suffocated on the street,
    with hands raised,
    "Don't shoot!"
    For Water Protectors,
    For Flint,
    For Women,
    For Refugees,
    For Hijab-wearing Sisters and their Brothers,
    For the Dreamers,

LORD God Almighty,
>   teach me how to pray
>   with my feet,

>   That I might become a drum major for justice,
>   To march around Jericho's walls
>   And monuments to White Supremacy,
>   Till they come tumbling down;
>   That I might say,
>   As did Mother Pollard to young Martin,
>   "My feets is tired, but my soul is rested."
>   And that You, LORD God Almighty,
>   May one day say to me,
>   "You have beautiful feet."

>   Amen.

The Spirit of the LORD is upon Me.

(Delivered April 20, 2017, in Durham, North Carolina, for the closing convocation at Duke Divinity School at Duke University.)

The Spirit of the LORD is upon me because the LORD has anointed me bring Good News to:

Those working three jobs, yet still living beneath the poverty line and struggling to make ends meet on minimum wage.

To entire communities, first redlined, now gentrified, property taxes rising, and grandmothers being displaced from their homes.

To those forced to choose daily between eating, filling their prescriptions, or keeping their lights on.

To those living in cars, in shelters, under bridges, to those with no shelter of their own who must seek rest on open couches.

To those whose medical expenses have depleted their savings.

To those living one missed paycheck from the streets.

To those whose only meals each day are free school breakfast and lunch, and who starve when the weekend comes.

To those living in communities afflicted by food apartheid.

To those whose prices are gouged and whose lenders are predatory.

The Spirit of the LORD is upon me because the LORD has anointed me proclaim Good News to bring an end to:

Mandatory minimum sentences
Prison bed quotas
For-profit prisons
The school-to-prison pipeline
Mass incarceration

The prison industrial complex
The War on Us

The Spirit of the LORD is upon me because the LORD has anointed me bring Good News to:

Sacred tribal lands threatened by pipelines

Bible studies bombarded by bullets

Jewish cemeteries desecrated and Jewish centers bomb threatened

Hijab-wearing sisters accosted and assaulted

Those who live in fear of the cold hands of ICE

Women not given equal pay for equal work

Cities with water tainted (or poisoned) with lead

To sisters yanked out of their vehicles for failure to use a turn signal, with knees at their neck poolside, wrestled to the ground while defending their assaulted sons, shot down while sleeping in their own beds

To brothers shot down while standing up with their hands up, shot down while lying down with their hands up, declared big and bad by helicopters hovering above, shot down with hands handcuffed, shot down at the park, shot down because their music is too loud, shot in the back while running away, shot down with Skittles and Iced Tea, shot down while jogging,

To brothers whose spines have been severed with knees on their necks who still cannot breathe.

The Spirit of the LORD is upon me because the LORD has anointed me bring Good News:

The Good News that no weapon formed against us shall prosper!

The Good News that weeping may endure for the night, but joy still comes in the morning!

The Good News that the lion will lie down with the Lamb!

The Good News that every valley shall be exalted, and every mountain and hill brought low, the crooked places shall be made straight and the rough places smooth; The glory of the LORD shall be revealed, and all flesh shall see it together!

The Good News that a change is gonna come!

The Good News that we shall overcome!

The Good News that the arc of the moral universe is long, but it still bends toward justice!

The Good News that *there is* a river whose streams shall make glad the city of God, the holy place of the tabernacle of the Most High. [That] God is in the midst of her, and she shall not be moved![4]

The Good News that swords shall be beaten into plowshares and spears into pruning hooks!

The Good News that all debts shall be canceled!

The Good News that God shall wipe every tear from every eye!

The Good News that "I'm messed up, Homie, you messed up, but if God's got us, then we gon' be all right!"

The Good News that we shall be free!

Free at last, free at last, thank God Almighty, we're free at last!

I Resist: A Prayer for the Nation

(Delivered November 1, 2017, in Washington, D.C., as the opening prayer for the United States House of Representatives.)

Immutable God, greater than all that has or ever will be conceived, hear our prayer:

For ancestors at rest in the abode of angels, accosted and assaulted while present upon these shores, unyielding avalanches of animus never atoned,

For babies bombarded by bombs, bounties placed upon their beautiful heads at birth,

For the cacophony of cries citing crimes against humanity, callous cycles of crisis, casualties colored in chalk.

In Your name, we shall resist evil by loving our neighbors as ourselves.

Grant that we become drum majors of justice, promulgators of peace, architects of an America freed from greed, hate, oppression, racism, suppression, indeed, the very threat of tyranny, replete with liberty and justice for all,

Till that great day when lions shall lie down with lambs and we study war no more, when justice flows like waters, and righteousness, like a mighty stream—

And all God's children are free,

Amen.

1619–Until

Enslave them.
Maim them.
Terrorize them.
Lynch them.
Drug them.
Rape them.
Stereotype them.
Separate them.
Bomb them.
Shoot them.
Profile them.
Surveil them.
Infiltrate them.
Mass incarcerate them.
Tell them to stop playing the victim.
Tell them to get over it.
Tell them it's their fault.
Then wash your hands of it all.

America,
1619–Until.

Today

(Penned at Kelly Ingram Park in Birmingham, Alabama, across the street from the Sixteenth Street Baptist Church that was bombed on September 15, 1963.)

Today I watched ...
Black and Brown children ...
At play in a park ...
Where years before ...
Young children were met ...
By fire hoses ...
And canines ...
Across from where ...
Four little girls ...
Died at church ...
From a bomb ...
Down the street from where ...
A little boy ...
Was shot in the back ...
By police ...
The same day ...
And though knowing ...
In America today ...
Black and Brown children ...
Are still are shot by police ...
In parks ...
Tamir Rice ...
Say his name ...

And though knowing ...
Bans and threats of a wall ...
Descend upon Brown people ...
Separating Brown children ...
From their families ...
I am grateful ...
That the arc still bends ...
Toward justice ...
If you have the courage ...
To bend it.

Amen.

I Believe.

I believe that healthcare is a human right.
I believe that Black lives matter.
I believe that truth crushed to the earth will rise again.
I believe in love.
I believe refugees are welcome.
I believe in the joy that cascades from every child's smile.
I believe in the wisdom of the Elders.
I believe in God.
I believe social distancing works.
I believe we will defeat this virus together.
I believe in hope.
I believe trouble don't last always.

I believe we will win.

Where Hope Is Found

Eternal God
We confess
That as casualties mount
And economies struggle
As schools close
And nations quarantine
As hospitals fill
And anxiety rises
That it is difficult
For us
To find hope
Still God
Amid it all
These are not
Hopeless times
For hope is found
In health workers
Who continue
To show up
To care
For their neighbors
In teachers
Who still love and reach students
In virtual spaces
In grocery store workers
Who keep shelves stocked
And stores cleaned

Yes, hope is found
In younger neighbors
Checking in
On older neighbors
And churches
That still make sure
Their neighbors are fed
Yes, hope is found
In our capacity
To show our love for You
Our love for ourselves
And our love for our neighbors
Even if
At a safe distance
Though it sometimes feels
Like the Earth
Is spinning off its axis
Hope is found
In knowing
That the Earth still spins
In the circumference of your hands
And that each day
The sun still rises
Again.
And so, shall we rise
Again.

Amen.

Dallas: America's Capital of Functional White Supremacy

On the morning of April 25, 2018, I sat in the chambers of the Dallas City Council expecting to bear witness to history. After a 122-year reign in the city of Dallas, it appeared that the council was about to vote to remove Dallas' oldest and tallest Confederate monument. Months of sustained activism and organizing had brought us here to the brink of change.

The previous summer, in July 2017, I had begun making social media posts calling for Dallas to bring down these monuments to white supremacy that littered our public spaces. The posts quickly gained momentum, and Dallas city councilman Philip Kingston courageously lent his support to the cause. Within a matter of weeks, Kingston drafted a resolution and got the signatures of other councilpersons to bring the monuments down. I, along with a coalition of scholars, faith leaders, and activists, mobilized to garner further support for this cause.

Almost as quickly as we had mobilized, opposition arose. Then Dallas mayor Michael S. Rawlings, who championed himself as a Southern progressive mayor, actively worked to slow and thwart our efforts. Instead of bringing the resolution to an immediate vote, he formed a task force to "study" the issue and to provide recommendations. Amazingly, most of Dallas' Black elected city council members jumped behind the mayor's plan and held a tragic press conference in support of it, suggesting that the monuments had been up for more than a century and that there was not a need to remove them immediately.

On August 10, 2017, I joined a small group of scholars, faith leaders, and activists on the grounds of the Confederate War Memorial for a rally calling for its immediate removal. I was invited to offer the closing address. When we arrived for the rally, three other groups were present, one being undercover Dallas police officers whose faces and names I had become familiar with over many years of protesting in the city. The second group was composed of media professionals, whom I had also gotten to known well over the years after several interviews related to our social justice pursuits. The third group was a mixture of white supremacist leaders and members representing groups ranging from the alt-right to the KKK. They, of course, had come in opposition to our rally.

The latter group stood silent for most of the rally. However, when it was time for me to speak, they advanced closer to our group and attempted to drown out my message with their shouts. Undaunted, I continued to speak, my voice rising louder in volume. I was determined to finish, and I refused to be silenced.

When I completed my words, I walked in the direction of these white supremacists. Before I knew it, we were face-to-face, surrounded by the officers, the media, and my colleagues in justice. Some people in the crowd called for us to dismiss and to disengage with these white supremacists, but as a student of the American civil rights movement, I knew that we had them right where we wanted them. As I spoke to them, I also spoke through them and past them to the ever-present cameras, posing simple questions regarding race and history that I knew they would be challenged to answer appropriately as they were being filmed.

Finally, I peppered each of them with this question: "What would have happened to my people had the South won?" One quickly responded, "I don't know." Another told me to listen to common sense and began to share off topic about how poor his white family was. Continuing with the trend of speaking off topic, another decided to share that President Lincoln was a tyrant that wanted to send all Blacks back to Africa.

I was certain that I had them now. I continued to advance my question before responding, "It's a simple question. The answer is that they would have remained in bondage." This declaration of truth placed them in even greater consternation. I then focused my attention on one man who was carrying a large Confederate flag. I asked him if he supported Lincoln's platform. He responded, "No." I then asked him why he carried that flag. He responded, "My family fought to save their farm under this flag." I quickly responded, "Who was working that farm?" He responded, "My family was. Do you know how much a slave cost back then?"

I had what I needed and walked away.

Some members of our group began singing "We Shall Overcome." The white supremacists retorted by singing a rendition of "Dixie."

A few months later, I received a message from Rabbi Andrew Paley of Temple Shalom in Dallas one Sunday night telling me to quickly turn on *Last Week Tonight with John Oliver*. Apparently, my interaction with these white supremacists had become a featured and memorable part of his segment on the Confederacy. This segment continues to go viral at least twice a year.

Following the Unite the Right rally in Charlottesville, Virginia, on August 12, 2017, led by Dallas native Richard Spencer, an activist group called In Solidarity organized the Rally to End White Supremacy in front of Dallas City Hall on August 19. During the Charlottesville rally, Heather Heyer, a young white woman marching in the streets for justice, was killed after a young white supremacist drove his vehicle into a crowd of marchers. Subsequently, over three thousand people showed up at the August 19 rally in Dallas to demand the removal of Confederate monuments. Again, I was invited to speak.

In response to my remarks, a chant broke out across the crowd, echoing, "Bring them down!" It was a glorious moment! Our collective momentum resulted in the Dallas City Council voting to remove the Lee monument from Lee Park on September 6. Having shunned the mayor's task force initially as a stall tactic, after this victory, I joined the task force with the intent of being an additional voice calling for the removal of all Confederate monuments in the city. After weeks of work on the task force, we offered a clear recommendation that all Confederate monuments be removed immediately from public spaces in Dallas. I also put forth a motion passed unanimously by the task force for Dallas to commission and erect a memorial to Allen Brooks at the sight of his 1910 lynching.

The council was supposed to act on our recommendations within a month. No action was taken for several months. In March 2018, when the matter came back before the council, the tone of some council members, including Mayor Rawlings, had changed once again. Some were now talking about "contextualizing" the Civil War Memorial by placing monuments to civil rights leaders around it. They even spoke of contextualizing it by placing a lynching marker at its base. Despite the sincere efforts of our task force and the clear recommendations that we offered, some members of the council seemed to be arguing for everything but the removal the monument. This was unacceptable.

Still, at the time, it seemed to matter little because a preliminary count of council votes had been taken. Purportedly, we still had the votes for removal. But as I sat in my chair the morning of April 25, I noticed that there was a lot of movement and conversation happening between councilpersons near their seats. Kingston looked distressed. A Black councilperson who had voiced his full support failed to look in our coalition's direction. That is when I received a text message: "We lost him."

I sat in utter dismay as the issue of the monument's removal formally returned to the floor. I sat in horror as I listened to our

Black councilpersons conflate Dr. King's work with a call to unify Dallas together by not bringing down the monument. Some questioned that if we brought the monument down, how could we learn from it? I thought to myself that if we had not learned from it over the past 122 years, what did we hope to *learn* from it now?

Unfortunately, there is historical precedence for such accommodationist Black leadership in Dallas. An entire book called *The Accommodation: The Politics of Race in an American City* by Jim Schutze was published concerning it in 1986. The book documented how the white business establishment in Dallas co-opted Black leaders in Dallas during the days of the American civil rights movement to quell uprisings for justice and equality in the city. Black pastors, such as the members of the Interdenominational Ministerial Alliance, openly disparaged and undermined Black protest and even opposed the screening of a movie in Dallas celebrating the life of Dr. King after his assassination. The racial truths revealed by *The Accommodation* were so vigorously opposed by the white business establishment that they were able to ultimately persuade the book's initial publisher to drop it.

As I sat in the chambers that day, I had the uneasy feeling that I was bearing witness to *The Accommodation 2.0.*

A Black city councilman put forth a motion to table the matter indefinitely. The purpose of the motion was clear: to kill the issue without officially voting against it. Three of the four Black councilpersons voted in favor of the motion. Had they all voted in favor of the removal the monument instead, it would have been taken down.

I remained stunned and sat in near silence for much of the remainder of the day. I marveled in anguish at the lingering power of white supremacy in Dallas and questioned whether Black political power really existed in the city. Who truly held the power behind those seats, such that Black men representing Black majority districts would vote to uphold the legacy of the Confederacy in Dallas?

Providentially, that same day, the Urban Institute released its report titled "Inclusive Recovery in US Cities." The report, the "first empirical analysis of how economic health and inclusion interact in US cities over several decades," ranked Dallas dead last out of 274 American cities with a population of one hundred thousand or more residents in terms of racial segregation and racial inequity. Here was empirical evidence that there is something in the water in the city of Dallas. Here was empirical evidence denoting Dallas as the capital of functional white supremacy in America.

But how did we get here?

* * * * *

On the morning of May 24, 1841, General Edward Tarrant, brigadier general of the Fourth Brigade, a northeast Texas militia, led his forces to attack the Caddo Nation near Village Creek. Tarrant, a prosperous Texas slave master and landowner in Red River County, was not new to engaging in such aggressions. He had led forces to attack and massacre Indigenous people for two decades. This attack, however, would be his last.

Along the banks of the river known to the Caddo as the Arkikosa, Tarrant and his militia murdered the Caddo natives and burned down their skillfully made huts that proudly stood near the river's bank. From there, the militia continued north along the river and continued their rampage, murdering other Indigenous people and burning down their homes. The surviving Caddos were forced to move westward. Soon, new white settlements were erected on this stolen land.

A millennium prior, around 800 C.E., the Caddo people had arrived at the Village Creek region from the Mississippi Valley. Their total territory extended from Texas to include portions of Oklahoma, Arkansas, and Louisiana. The Caddos created a thriving and sophisticated society. They built mound-styled homes covered in grass, they hunted bear, deer, and buffalo, and they harvested corn, beans, squash, and other crops. At the height of their society, the Caddos numbered over two hundred fifty thousand.

When the Spanish arrived in Texas, they were greeted by the Caddo people with proclamations of "taychas!" which means "friend." The Spaniards later came to call the Caddo people the "Tejas," and Tejas became Texas. Disappointingly, the Republic of Texas did not regard the Caddo people as friends. For the two decades after they were removed from their homeland along the Arkikosa, the Caddos continued to be forced westward and face additional white aggression. By 1859, the Caddo population numbered one thousand.

Among the members of Tarrant's militia that attacked and massacred the Caddo people that fateful Monday in May 1841 was a man named John Neely Bryan. After clearing the Caddo people from the land, Bryan remained in the area and began a new white settlement that same year. The following year, a young Black man named Smith became the first enslaved person to arrive, the property of the Mabel Gilbert family that settled the area. In 1846, Bryan helped organize what is now Dallas County. In 1856, Bryan's settlement, called the City of Dallas, was incorporated. By 1859, 678 whites and ninety-seven enslaved Blacks made up the city's population.

Bryan served in the Confederate army during the American Civil War, returning early from war because of age and poor health. He later became a leading advocate for reinstating full political rights to former Confederate soldiers, an important precursor to the premature end to the Reconstruction Era, which was intended to grant political and economic rights to the newly emancipated Blacks.

By 1860, Dallas had grown into a small town that was heavily dependent on cotton as well as the slave labor that it required. On July 8 of that year, a fire destroyed much of downtown Dallas, and it was rumored that abolitionist ministers from the North had incited a slave rebellion in the city. On July 24, near the banks of the Arkikosa, "Uncle Cato" Miller, Patrick Jenkins, and Samuel Smith, each enslaved Blacks, were lynched in retaliation.

These three men were not the first Blacks to be lynched in Dallas. That dubious distinction belongs to a Black woman named Jane Elkins. She had been convicted of murdering her white master as he attempted to rape her—again. Elkins was hanged on May 17, 1853, on the property that had belonged to John Neely Bryan before he gifted it to Dallas County.

On June 25, 1896, the cornerstone of the Confederate War Memorial was dedicated in Dallas, only a month after the US Supreme Court's infamous *Plessy* v. *Ferguson* ruling, which codified white supremacy nationally and gave rise to the myth of "separate but equal." On April 29, 1897, before a crowd of thousands, including Confederate veterans and Texas governor Charles Allen Culberson, the monument was dedicated. At the time it was erected, the Confederate War Memorial was the largest structure erected in Dallas County, standing six stories tall and in view of the Arkikosa, now known as the Trinity River.

The random lynching of Black people perceived to be guilty of a crime continued into the twentieth century. On March 3, 1910, Allen Brooks was lynched at the corner of Akard and Main Street in downtown Dallas before five thousand men, women, and children. That morning, a mob had broken into a second-floor courtroom at the Dallas County Courthouse and overtaken the authorities. They tied a noose around Brooks's neck and threw the other end of the rope down to the mob gathered on the lawn. The waiting mob pulled the rope with such force that Mr. Brooks's body broke the window frame. He landed on his head and was dragged by the noose around his neck for a half mile. The friction caused by his body dragging over the road was so intense that his clothing was ripped from his body. Pieces of Brooks's tattered garments were divided among the crowd as souvenirs. After the lynching, trains at the downtown Union Station were stopped as the lynch mob descended upon the station, intent on hanging any Black person who detrained.

The city continued to nurture the climate of racial hatred that marked its founding. At the beginning of the twentieth century, the city of Dallas boasted the largest Ku Klux Klan chapter in America. At its height, one out of every three eligible white men in Dallas were members of Klavern number 66. Dr. Hiram Wesley Evans, a Dallas dentist, joined Dallas' Klan chapter in 1920 and quickly ascended to the chapter's top leadership position. Evans personally participated in acts of violence against Black people, including the torture of a Black porter who worked at the Adolphus Hotel downtown. The Klan believed the porter was guilty of fraternizing with white women, so they kidnapped him from the hotel lobby and took him to the Trinity River Bottoms, where acts of racial terror took place in Dallas for decades. There, the Klan beat him, blindfolded him, and tied a noose around his neck to make him think that he was going to be lynched. Ultimately, the Klan carved KKK into his head with acid before dropping him— bloodied, bruised, and bludgeoned—back at the Adolphus.

In November 1922, Dr. Evans became the Third Imperial Wizard of the Knights of the Ku Klux Klan in America—their national leader. Under Evans' leadership, on October 24, 1923— "Klan Day" at the State Fair of Texas in Dallas—the Klan hosted the single largest initiation of members in American history. Discounts for entry into the fair were given to all Klan members who arrived wearing their hood and sheet. An estimated 160,000 Klansmen attended the festivities. That evening, 25,000 members hosted the initiation ceremony, adding 5,631 men and 800 women to their ranks. At the event, Evans delivered an address titled "The Menace of Modern Immigration." Accordingly, Blacks were banned from the fairgrounds for the next thirteen years. Once allowed to return, it was only for a so-called "Negro Achievement Day" once a year, where they were still denied full access to the fair's amenities.

On June 12, 1936, President Franklin Delano Roosevelt helped unveil and dedicate a Confederate monument to General Robert E. Lee in a ceremony at Dallas' Lee Park. Also in attendance was D. W. Griffith, director of the groundbreaking 1915 film *Birth of a Nation*, the first film ever shown at the White House. The full-length movie glorified the KKK and contributed to new outbreaks of racial violence leading to the Red Summer of 1919. It also helped to swell the KKK's ranks and positioned them to seize political control of state houses across the nation.

President Roosevelt was in Dallas to attend the Texas Centennial Exposition festivities at the Texas State Fair. Notably, the Hall of Negro Life, erected at the state fair to honor the contributions of Blacks in America during the Centennial, was torn down by the city of Dallas. The Hall featured Black achievements in education, agriculture, medicine, business, and the arts, and each person who visited received a free copy of Du Bois's *What the Negro Has Done for the United States and Texas*. Many white attendees were made uncomfortable by seeing expressions of Black intelligence, and so the hall was not allowed to remain.

Many elected officials, judges, policemen, ministers, and businessmen were members of Dallas' KKK chapter. R. L. Thornton was among them. In 1916, Thornton founded Stiles, Thornton, and Lund, a banking company in Dallas known as the Mercantile National Bank. He served as its president until 1947. During the Great Depression, the bank organized the Dallas County State Bank, which became one of the national banks notorious for helping to establish redlining as policy across the nation, including Dallas. Dallas released its redlining map in 1937.

Thornton held other notable business positions in insurance, railroads, steel, utilities, and hotels across the years. He served as president of the Rotary Club of Dallas, president of the Dallas Chamber of Commerce (1933 to 1936), and president of the State Fair of Texas from 1945 to 1960. Thornton served as mayor of

Dallas from 1953 to 1961, the second longest term in the city's history.

In 1929, the first bombs were exploded at homes to terrorize Blacks attempting to move into South Dallas and to reinforce segregation lines. Over twenty years of terroristic bombings were carried out by white neighborhood and church groups against Black residents in South Dallas. These bombings resulted in almost no prosecutions or convictions for the crimes.

On July 12, 1951, the *Dallas Morning News* ran an article titled "New Negro Home Wrecked by Bomb." The article read,

> A dynamite bomb Wednesday night wrecked the back end of a new Negro bungalow that had just been completed at 4 p.m. at 4622 Meadow, near the Oakland intersection. It broke the uneasy peace in the South Dallas race situation which had existed since the city a few weeks ago asked in the Federal Bureau of Investigation and the Texas Rangers.

A bomb exploded in Dallas on July 7, 1950, that was so powerful it earned the distinction as the most powerful bomb of the year in America. Thirteen years later, when Dr. Martin Luther King Jr. came to Dallas to offer an address near South Dallas, the event was delayed because of a bomb threat.

President John F. Kennedy would be assassinated in Dallas later that year on November 22, 1963. However, well before Kennedy arrived, Dallas had already earned the distinction of being the "City of Hate." The city's reputation for threatened and actualized violence had moved Secret Service members to request that President Kennedy travel in his motorcade with bulletproof glass over his vehicle. Kennedy declined.

In the early 1950s, many Black homes in the North Park community of Dallas were seized by eminent domain, purportedly for the expansion of Love Field Airport. Instead, many of these homes and properties were simply given to white families.

In the 1960s, the State Fair of Texas began a campaign to seize Black homes due to market research that showed that white fairgoers were frightened by the sight of poor Black people along the route to the fair's entrance. In 1966, fair officials hired a consultant to help resolve their Negro problem. The consultant concluded that the land around Fair Park should be "bought up and turned into a paved, lighted, fenced parking lot" that would "eliminate the problem from sight." The report stated, "If the poor Negroes in their shacks cannot be seen, all the [white] guilt feelings ... will disappear, or at least be removed from primary consideration."

On May 8, 1987, an infield US congressional hearing was held in Dallas "to examine whether the Dallas police were using excessive force against minority citizens"—this after decades of police killings of unarmed Blacks and Latinos. Just fifteen years prior, in 1972, nine Black men had been killed and eleven others wounded by the Dallas Police Department in a matter of months. On July 24, 1973, a twelve year-old Latino boy named Santos Rodriguez was executed by a Dallas police officer who loaded his gun and played Russian roulette with his head, all over an allegation that he stole something from a vending machine. His brother David, who was also being interrogated in that Dallas police cruiser, had his feet soaked in his brother's blood while seated in the back seat. The officer served just two and a half years of a five-year sentence. By the mid-1980s, Dallas had the highest rate of per capita killings of residents by police in America. From 1973–2019, no Dallas police officer was convicted of the murder of a Dallas resident.

Over a period of twenty-six years, from 1990¬–2016, concentrated racial communities of poverty in Dallas doubled from 18 communities to 36. Today there are more racially concentrated communities of poverty in Dallas than in any other American city. From 2000–2012, poverty in Dallas increased by more than 40 percent. Today, 83 percent of the poor in Dallas are either Black or Latino. The greatest indicator of social determinants of health in Dallas is whether you live north or south of I-30, in a city still largely segregated along racial lines with Black and Brown people living primarily south and whites living primarily north. Life expectancy rates between zip codes—75215 (South Dallas) and 75204 (Uptown)—differ by nearly twenty-four years.

It is for all these reasons and many more that Dallas is the capital of functional white supremacy in America. And, again, white supremacy comes with a body count. When reflecting on the possibilities of Dallas' future given these harsh realities, the *Dallas Morning News* summarized the future of Dallas as young, Brown, and poor.

On January 9, 2019, I gathered with a group of Black pastors at our church's empowerment center in South Dallas. We were a newly formed group of Dallas-based Black activist pastors who had been doing justice work apart from one another for years but were being drawn together at this moment in Dallas' history to push for change. As we gathered, we were fully prepared to go to jail that day for the cause of justice if necessary. We were not a formal organization, but we had an agenda for change; thus, we named ourselves the Dallas Black Clergy Agenda.

I previously had served for several years as chair of Dallas' Martin Luther King Jr. Community Center, the nation's second King Center after the original based in Atlanta. I and another pastor, the Reverend Dr. Frederick D. Haynes III, had been invited to offer prayer and to speak during a wreath-laying for Dr. King at Dallas City Hall. Weeks prior, as we met together as pastors, we had made the decision to use this moment as an opportunity to lay out a moral agenda for Dallas and to challenge the elected officials we knew would be present there to pursue that agenda.

It was standing room only at Dallas City Hall that morning, and the program proceeded as planned. I offered a written prayer titled "Holy Soles." Dr. Haynes delivered a powerful address that lifted the legacy of Dr. King and called out Dallas' failures to manifest King's dream in the life of all its residents. As Dr. Haynes concluded, we all quickly advanced toward the podium. Initially, people thought this was just a part of Dr. Haynes's presentation.

They quickly learned differently.

We each took a part in issuing our demands to the Dallas city council members who were present. The Reverend Edwin Robinson, a brilliant organizer in Dallas, had provided exceptional leadership in shaping the language of our collective demands. We read the demands as follows:

> We demand that our city grant the requests of North Texans for Historical Justice, In Solidarity, Faith Forward Dallas and Faith in Texas to remove any and all monuments, plaques, and the like celebrating the Confederacy and our country's war on the freedom and equality of people of color, and Black people particularly, from public view on all public property excluding inside museums documenting the real and honest history of our city, state, and country.

> We are demanding complete and proper funding and resources for the Civilian Police Review Board as proposed by community organizations Mothers Against Police Brutality, Next Generation Action Network, the ACLU of Texas, and Faith Forward Dallas. This action will not just ensure that we have a true civilian-led police oversight committee in word, but they will have the resources to do the work for which they are commissioned in deed.

> We demand that our city support the work of Bianca and Derek Avery and Faith in Texas through instituting form-based code as the zoning policy for the entire city. This will relax the zoning policies and allow developers to build affordable housing

units for Dallas. Further, we request a public-private community partnership for oversight, strengthening the checks-and-balances responsibilities of the city's planning and zoning office. This will put the land back into the hands of the local community in a quicker, more responsible way.

We demand that all private and public employees have access to earned paid sick leave as laid out in the Working Texans for Paid Sick Leave platform and advanced by Workers Defense Project, Texas Organizing Project, Faith in Texas, and the AFL-CIO.

We are demanding the minimum wage rise significantly to be equivalent to the necessary living wage for all of our citizens using the MIT Dallas County Living Wage Calculator. Paying full-time workers a wage that keeps them mired in poverty is wrong and should not be the Dallas way. When low-wage workers get a boost, the extra money flows to their communities in short order. Businesses benefit when more working people can afford their products and services.

During our protest, we invited other clergy present to join us at the podium and stand with us in solidarity with our demands. Our numbers at the podium swelled swiftly and dramatically, and we refused to leave the platform and to turn the program back over to event organizers until we received a response from the councilpersons present. Mainly, we wanted their assurance that they would meet with us and place our demands on the council agenda for a vote. For some issues, like the Confederate monument, this was the only way to force the council to act.

Some police officers, undercover and uniformed, began to carefully approach where we stood. But we were prepared to go to jail if necessary, and we continued to hold the space. Finally, after a brief stalemate, some councilpersons agreed to meet with us, and we allowed the event to proceed.

For my participation in this direct action protest, I was disinvited as the keynote speaker for the following week's ninetieth birthday observance for Dr. King at the King Center. News of the withdrawn invitation reached the city's evening news. Councilperson Kingston investigated the matter and posted on social media: "After checking with those close to the decision, I believe this is pure retaliation, and it's outrageous that city appointees would engage in such illiberal and nasty behavior."

For me, being disinvited for standing up for what Dr. King stood up for proved to be one of the greatest affirmations of my call and ministry that I ever had received. I was emboldened.

Over the next several months, after our direct action and subsequent meetings with various council members, the Dallas City Council considered and voted on several issues of critical importance toward bringing greater equity to several historically neglected constituencies in our city. After tabling the matter indefinitely, on February 13, 2019, the Dallas City Council voted 11–4 to remove the Confederate War Memorial. On April 24, 2019, the Dallas City Council voted 10–4 to pass the Earned Paid Sick Time Ordinance, granting earned paid sick leave to all employees who work in the city limits of Dallas (after failing pass the same measure the previous year).

Also on April 24, the Dallas City Council voted unanimously to expand the power of the Police Oversight Board and to create a position for a police monitor to complete investigations and report the findings to board members. This was the first substantive change to the board in decades. Many of the changes were first advocated for during the congressional hearing on police brutality in Dallas that had been held in the city thirty-two years prior.

The moral arc of the universe is long, but it bends toward justice. But only if you bend it.

After years of deflections, delays, and denials, our collective action had brought swift changes in the city of Dallas.

There was much work left to be accomplished, but what we had accomplished together could not be underestimated. Although there long has been something in the water of Dallas, generations of brutalities enacted near the banks of the Arkikosa—something that has allowed functional white supremacy to reign—this was a sign that Dallas could change.

It was also a clear reminder of the actions that sometimes must be engaged to bring about change.

LAMENTS AND PUBLIC LITURGIES

Something in the Water!
John 7:37–38

(Delivered April 28, 2019, in Virginia Beach, Virginia, during the pop-up church service of the Something in the Water Festival)

Lament.

Four hundred years ago, there was something in the water.

It was us, it was our ancestors, kidnapped from the Mother Continent, bound with chains, shoved deep in the hulls of ships named Jesus, Hope, and Desire. The first twenty ancestors landed in 1619, were brought across these Atlantic waters, docked an hour northwest in Jamestown.

There was something else in the water. Our bodies, the bodies of our ancestors, tossed overboard into watery graves that muted their cries. Kidnappers could not collect on a sick body, but they could collect on lost cargo, so overboard we went.

Ever since, there has been something in the water. Something toxic concocted from the decay of the bodies callously thrown overboard. Let's call it hate. Let's call it denying the humanity of all God's creations. Let's call it forsaking the image of God present in every human countenance. Let's call it evil.

This something in the water has caused the theft of Native lands. This something in the water has caused the lynching of Black and Brown bodies.

Peer into the water. Do you see it?

Looks like mass incarceration.

Looks like children in cages.

Looks like Flint.

Looks like Standing Rock.

Looks like nine Black bodies bombarded by bullets in Bible study.

Looks like three Black churches burned down in Louisiana.

Looks like redlining.

Looks like the Tuskegee experiment.

Looks like Charlottesville.

Looks like Emmett Till.

There's something in the water.

Sounds like Eric Garner—I can't breathe!

Sounds like Michael Brown—hands up, don't shoot!

Sounds like Tamir Rice.

Sounds like Botham Jean.

Sounds like Sandra Bland.

Sounds like Rekia Boyd.

Sounds like Walter Scott.

Sounds like Freddie Gray.

Sounds like Antwon Rose.

Sounds like hashtag, hashtag, hashtag, hashtag, hashtag...

Sounds like the cries of a mother with three jobs who can't afford to feed her child. Sounds like self-hate. Sounds like pulling the trigger on another Brother in the set: Nipsey Hussle, rest in peace.

In Lament, we hear the cry of the prophet Habakkuk: "How long, O LORD, must I call for help? But you do not listen! 'Violence is everywhere!' I cry, but you do not come to save."[5]

We hear Billie Holiday's cry: "Scent of magnolias, sweet and fresh. Then the sudden smell of burning flesh. Strange fruit!"

We hear Pac's cry: "I suffered through the years and shed so many tears. Lord, I lost so many peers, and shed so many tears."[6]

We hear Marvin Gaye's cry: "Makes me want to holla, throw up my hands. Makes me want to holla, through up my hands!"[7]

There's something in the water!

Let the track breathe.

Resist.

There's something in the water. It's still us. It is our ancestors.

"Wade in the water. Wade in the water, children. Wade in the water. God's gonna trouble the water."[8]

The water is our refuge. The water is our resistance. The water hides our scent from masters and bloodhounds on our track.

Yes, we resist!

We resist everything that seeks to rob us of our full humanity. We resist everything that seeks to erase our epistemology.

We are created in the image of God! We, too, sing America, Langston Hughes. We are created in the image of God. We are created in the image of God. We are created in the image of God.

We were not born slaves, but kings and queens. Our ancestors gave birth to astronomy, philosophy, medicine, and theology.

We resist! So, we build underground railroads to freedom. We resist. So, we build our own churches!

We resist, so we build our own schools!

We resist. So, we build up our children! We resist! So, we build our own businesses! Burn them down and we build them back ... again!

There's something in the water. Looks like Moses in the Nile. Looks like the Children of Israel crossing the Red Sea. Looks like the Children of Israel crossing the Jordan. Looks like Jesus walking on the water.

There's something in the water! Take me to the water to be baptized!

There's something in the water. Looks like Sojourner Truth. Looks like Ida B. Wells. Looks like Malcolm X. Looks like Fannie Lou Hamer. Looks like Coretta Scott King.

There's something in the water. Looks like my momma. Looks like my daddy. Looks like Montgomery. Looks like Birmingham. Looks like Selma. Looks like Ferguson.

Sounds like, "Pharaoh, let my people go!"

Sounds like, "No weapon formed against me shall prosper!"

Sounds like, "Ain't gonna let nobody turn me around, turn me around, turn me around, ain't gonna let nobody turn me around. I'm gonna keep on walkin', keep on talkin', marching down to freedom land!"

Sounds like, "But we have this treasure in earthen vessels. We are pressed on every side by troubles, but we are not crushed. We are perplexed, but not driven to despair. We are hunted down, but never abandoned by God. We get knocked down, but we are not destroyed."[9]

Let the track breathe.

Hope.

There's something in the water. We are a people of hope because of something in the water. The Spirit of God is in the water. It is the Spirit that has brought us to this place, the very place were our ancestors were brought in chains.

Yes, we know lament.

Yes, we must resist.

But we are a people of hope.

"It's been a long, a long time coming, but I know, a change gon' come. Yes, it will!"[10]

We are a people of hope guided by the North Star to liberty!

We are a people of hope, speaking those things that are not as though they were.[11]

We are a people of hope, co-laboring with God to reimagine our society.

We are Dr. King's promise: "I may not get there with you, but we as a people will get it to the promised land!"[12]

We are Maya Angelou's pupils. Out of the huts of history's shame, we rise! Up from a past that's rooted in pain, we rise! We are a black ocean, leaping and wide, welling and swelling, we bear in the tide. We rise! We rise! We rise!

We are Tupac's rose that grew up from concrete!

There is something in the water. Hope is in the water. The Spirit is in the water.

We believe truth crushed to the earth will rise again!

We believe the arc of the moral universe is long, but it bends toward justice!

We will create a world free of racism, xenophobia, war, and poverty, where zip codes do not determine your life expectancy. Where mass shootings cease, and where healthcare is a human right.

We have the audacity of hope! We believe there is still something in the water that can turn water to wine.

We believe in a God who has spoken, "For I know the plans I have for you. They are plans for good and not for disaster, to give you a hope and a future."

There is something in the water, for the Bible says, "On the last day, the climax of the festival, Jesus stood and shouted to the crowds, 'Anyone who is thirsty may come to me. Anyone who believes may come and drink. Rivers of living water will flow from the heart!'"

Yes, there's something in the water! There's power in the water. There's deliverance in the water. There's salvation in the water. There's healing in the water!

So, let justice flow like waters, and righteousness, like a mighty stream!

That's why we won't wait until the battle is over. We will shout right now!

For a Psalmist from Virginia and a prophet from Compton have told us,

We gon' be all right!

If God be for us, who can be against us!

There's something in the water!

Why We March

(An editorial published in *The Huffington Post* on June 18, 2017.)

Tomorrow morning, a diverse coalition of North Texans will gather in downtown Dallas to march. What would compel this body to exchange a lazy Saturday morning for a public demonstration in the streets? For what purpose would they forgo the creature comfort of air-conditioning to assemble under an oppressive summer sun?

The answer may be best expressed in names: Jordan Edwards. Santos Rodriguez. Fred Bradford Jr. Ahjah Dixon. James Harrison. Clinton Allen. Etta Collins.

The names move well beyond the plane of North Texas and echo from cities and municipalities across the nation: Eric Garner. Michael Brown Jr. Sandra Bland. Freddie Gray. Alton Sterling. Rekia Boyd. Philando Castile. Terence Crutcher. Walter Scott. Tamir Rice.

And this abbreviated list does not begin to scratch the surface. The literal and the metaphorical beat of police brutality simply goes on and on and on.

To be clear, the March to End Police Brutality is not a protest against law enforcement. This must be stated emphatically in this current social and political climate, as some deem support of police and opposition to police brutality as mutually exclusive. They are not. Our march is not against police, but rather against the policing and justice system that continues to find creative ways not to convict officers for their callous crimes.

The prosecution of a police officer for killing a Black man is a rare occurrence. The last year that a Dallas police officer was sentenced in the death of a Dallas citizen was 1973. That officer—Darrell Cain—literally played Russian roulette with a youth's head for the alleged crime of stealing from a vending machine. He served less than three years of a five-year sentence.

It is undeniable that our policing and justice systems are broken. They are so defunct that even when these crimes against humanity are caught on camera, a conviction is seldom brought forward. That is, on those occasions when the actual camera footage is released.

Nearly two months after former Balch Springs, Texas officer Roy Oliver aimed his rifle and took the life of young Jordan Edwards, the camera footage had not been released to the public. While awaiting information, Edwards' mother and father had the added pain of experiencing Mother's Day and Father's Day without their son. Meanwhile, Oliver's attorneys began using the media to prepare its defense: post-traumatic stress disorder.

Based upon the stream of acquittals nationwide, Oliver's fifteen-year sentence was a historic reversal of the trend, but this has not been the norm. On April 21, 2017, former Dallas police officer Bryan Burgess was found not guilty in the death of Fred Bradford Jr. On May 2, that same year, the United States Department of Justice decided not to pursue federal charges against Baton Rouge police officers Blane Salamoni and Howie Lake II in the death of Alton Sterling. On May 18, Tulsa police officer Betty Jo Shelby was found not guilty in the death of Terence Crutcher. Less than one month later, on June 16, Minnesota officer Jeronimo Yanez was cleared of all charges in the shooting death of Philando Castile. The Sandra Bland Bill, signed into law by Texas Governor Greg Abbott on the day before the Castile case verdict was issued, was gutted by the Texas Legislature for the very issue that gave rise to former Texas state trooper Brian Encinia's infamous encounter with Bland. The law's provisions include that an officer should not arrest someone for committing a ticket-able offense, while granting measures that mandate "county jails divert people with mental health and substance abuse issues toward treatment, [make] it easier for defendants to receive a personal bond if they have a mental illness or intellectual disability, and [require] that independent law enforcement agencies investigate jail deaths."

Yes, the beat goes on. And so, we march.

We march to magnify the stain of police brutality that thrives when good people remain silent.

We march to place pressure upon the policing and judicial system and demonstrate that we refuse to normalize these injustices and that by all peaceful means necessary, we will hold them accountable, be it in the streets or at the ballot box. We march to encourage the endless stream of families who weep daily over the loss of their loved ones and remind them that they are not alone.

And we march with the confidence that, as Dr. King espoused, "the arc of the moral universe is long, but it bends toward justice." Though justice has been delayed, it will not forever be denied.

In his seminal text *Why We Can't Wait*, Dr. King wrote,

> Where, in the days of slavery, social license and custom placed the unbridled power of the whip in the hands of overseers and masters, today— especially in the southern half of the nation—armies of officials are clothed in uniform, invested with authority, armed with the instruments of violence and death and conditioned to believe that they can intimidate, maim or kill Negroes with the same recklessness that once motivated the slaveowner. If one doubts this conclusion, let him search the records and find how rarely in any southern state a police officer has been punished for abusing a Negro.

A half century after the publication of this text, the record remains clear. Thousands of names have been added to the fatal rolls of police brutality. Often, the culprits have walked free.

And so, we march, and we will continue to march, until justice flows like waters, and righteousness like a mighty stream.[13] '

Get Away, Jordan: A Eulogy for Jordan Edwards

(Delivered May 4, 2017, in Balch Springs, Texas,
at the vigil for Jordan Edwards.)

The name Jordan has rung forth with prophetic hope for many people over many generations.

The etymology of that name means "to descend" or to "flow down."

It speaks of the River Jordan that flows down from Israel to Jordan, that river which served as the entry point of the Hebrew people into their promised land. That same river whose waters served as a baptismal pool for the Christ. That same river, reimagined by my people upon American shores, who recast the mighty Ohio River as the Jordan, knowing that as soon as they crossed over, they would know liberty.

For the joys of liberty, my forebears penned their prophetic hope in subversive song:

Get away, Jordan!
Get away, Jordan!
Get away, Jordan!
I want to cross over to see my Lord.[14]

Yet, over the past week, the name Jordan has not rung out with joy or with prophetic hope. Instead, it has rung out with a palpable pain. As the name Jordan has rung out, our souls have cried out, "Oh God, not another hashtag!" As the name Jordan has rung out, our hearts have cried out, "Oh God, not more innocent blood spilled upon car seats!" As the name Jordan has rung out, we have lifted our voices communally toward Heaven to cry out, "How long, oh God, must we continue to endure the sting of police brutality?"

As the name Jordan has rung out, our hearts have been broken over and over, again. Even after the fact, our heart's desire has been to shield and to protect that young soul. And so, we have also cried aloud, "Get away, Jordan!"

"Get away from that party!"
"Get away, Jordan!"
"Get down the street!"
"Get away, Jordan!"
"Driver, drive swifter!"
"Get away, Jordan!"
"Get away from Oliver's gun!"

But Jordan is no more. Still, he did get away. Away from the ills of this world. Away from the racism passed down from generation to generation as America's greatest inheritance. Away from evil itself.

Jordan crossed over to see his Lord.

So, rest on, sweet Prince Jordan. We will see you on the other side. While we remain present on this side, though it stings, we will continue to call forth your name. And we shall continue to pursue justice for you and for all who have fallen to police brutality. Your living—and your dying—will not be in vain.

We shall continue to pursue justice until justice flows down like river waters, and righteousness like a mighty stream.[15]

A Brief Translation of What Folks Actually Mean When They Oppose Our Resistance

(An editorial published in *The Huffington Post* on January 24, 2017.)

Here is a brief translation of what folks really mean when they oppose our resistance:

1. "We need unity. You are causing division."
   Translation: Silence your dissent.

2. "You are overreacting. Things won't be that bad."
   Translation: "My privilege isolates me from any known harm. Oh yeah, and silence your dissent."

3. "Just pray for our leaders."
   Translation: "Silence your dissent."

4. "You are not acting like an American."
   Translation: "I am conveniently forgetting that this nation was born in protest. I am also conveniently forgetting that I have been outspoken and protesting continuously for years because things are the way I want them now."
   "Oh, and silence your dissent."

5. "You're racist."
   Translation: "I am deflecting. I am a racist. Silence your dissent."

6. "Jesus and Dr. King would not approve."
   Translation: "I prefer my Jesus and Dr. King nice and sanitized, without all that turning-over-tables and shutting-cities-down stuff. Silence your dissent."

7. "People change. Give him a chance."
   Translation: "My cognitive dissonance won't allow me to see what is actually taking place. I despise you for pointing out the inconsistencies between my beliefs and reality. Silence your dissent."

8. "Shut up and stop your complaining!"
   Translation: "I'm a mean and insensitive person. Silence your dissent."

   Friends, don't silence your dissent.
   Resist.
   Stay woke.
   Keep speaking up.
   Keep standing up for justice.

"Freedom is never voluntarily given by the oppressor; it must be demanded by the oppressed." —Dr. Martin Luther King Jr.

Wake Up and Stay Woke!
Acts 20:7–12

(Delivered September 29, 2016, in Dallas, Texas, during the opening
worship service of the North Texas Annual Conference of the African
Methodist Episcopal Church)

The final scene of legendary filmmaker Spike Lee's cinematic
classic, *School Daze*, features an intense student, Dap (a role
exquisitely played by the equally legendary Laurence Fishburne),
as he sprints across the campus courtyard of the fictional
Mission College. After running for some distance and hurdling
a wall, Dap finally makes his way to the center of the courtyard.
There, the character looks directly into the camera lens to
declare a two-word imperative: "Wake up!"

This singular message is repeated by Dap thirteen times in less
than two minutes during the final three and a half minutes of the
film. As Dap continues to shout this refrain, the entire campus is
stirred from their slumber. Mission students, faculty, staff, and
administrators begin to flood the courtyard, now awake, standing
together side by side. At the fourteenth and final declaration, with
the entire campus surrounding him, Dap offers a slight deviation
in his declaration. Dap now utters a plea: "Please, wake up."
With these words, the film ends with a still frame, accompanied
by the unmistakable sound of a ringing alarm clock.

It is well-known that being asleep when one should be
awake can bring tragic consequences. Falling asleep on the job
can quickly result in a termination. Falling asleep in class can
quickly result in missing vital information needed to pass the
course. Falling asleep while operating heavy machinery or while
driving a vehicle can prove fatal not only for the driver but for
other passengers or people in surrounding automobiles. To keep
us from falling asleep at the wrong time, we are warned against
the use of certain medications at certain times, as their chemical
properties can make one drowsy and prone to slumber.

What is true in a physical sense also is true regarding social awareness. Just as it's dangerous to be asleep at certain times, it's also dangerous to be in a social slumber during seasons of critical importance. Being asleep means not being attentive, alert, or active. In times like these, not being attentive, alert, or active can have fatal consequences. It's imperative that we all be awake—or, as stated in the vernacular of these times, that we "stay woke."

We must stay woke to wealth disparity. *The Wall Street Journal* reported in 2016 that it would take 228 years for the average Black family to amass the wealth of an average white family.[16] We must stay woke politically. The current occupant of the White House demonstrated such hatred, racism, and xenophobia that it won him the endorsement of the Ku Klux Klan. We must stay woke as it relates to police brutality. Although young Black men ages fifteen to twenty-nine only make up 2 percent of the American population, they account for over 15 percent of all police-related deaths.

We must stay woke about education. Here in Texas, the state Board of Education is constantly seeking to rewrite history by approving textbooks for our young people that call enslaved Africans unpaid workers and Mexican migrants lazy, and then go so far as to suggest that the American system of chattel slavery was really not all that bad. We must stay woke in Dallas, for while we have the nation's fastest-growing business district, we also lead all major American cities in our level of childhood poverty.

We must stay woke because so many young Black men are dying in our city that one news outlet began a series called "Dying in Dallas." We must stay woke because our AME Annual Conference is meeting less than two miles from what the FBI claims is the most dangerous intersection in the entire state.

Yet, even with all these factors at work, both locally and nationally, I submit an even greater concern: In times like these—when being dormant can have fatal consequences—it often appears as if the church is in a deep slumber. Despite the clear mandate that we stay woke in this world, there is mounting evidence that we are fast asleep. The church often appears to be asleep to the shifting paradigms of our society and of our world.

Twenty-five years before Spike Lee's seminal film was released, a fellow Morehouse man spoke prophetically from a Birmingham jail cell. Armed with only a pen and the margins of a newspaper (and, later, scraps of paper smuggled to him by his attorney), the Reverend Dr. Martin Luther King Jr. penned what is widely considered to be the greatest treatise on nonviolent philosophy and resistance in the twentieth century. From his masterful text, we inherit such powerful quotations as "injustice anywhere is a threat to justice everywhere ... We are caught in an inescapable network of mutuality, tied in a single garment of destiny. Whatever affects one directly, affects all indirectly."

But even more compelling than Dr. King's words in defense of nonviolent resistance are his words in critique of the church: The contemporary church is so often a weak, ineffectual voice with an uncertain sound. It's so often the arch supporter of the status quo. Far from being disturbed by the presence of the church, the power structure of the average community is consoled by the church's often vocal sanction of things as they are. But the judgment of God is upon the church as never before. If the church of today does not recapture the sacrificial spirit of the early church, it will lose its authentic ring, forfeit the loyalty of millions, and be dismissed as an irrelevant social club with no meaning for the twentieth century. I meet young people every day whose disappointment with the church has risen to outright disgust.

Two years after his "Letter from Birmingham Jail," in his June 1965 commencement address at Oberlin College, Dr. King recounted the mythological story of Rip Van Winkle, who was asleep for twenty years and slept through the entire American Revolutionary War. To this, Dr. King stated, "There are all too many people who, in some great period of social change, fail to achieve the new mental outlooks that the new situation demands. There is nothing more tragic than to sleep through a revolution."

Later, at the National Cathedral in Washington D.C. in 1968, Dr. King elaborated on this theme: "One of the great liabilities of history is that all too many people fail to remain awake through great periods of social change. Every society has its protectors of status quo and its fraternities of the indifferent who are notorious for sleeping through revolutions. Today, our very survival depends on our ability to stay awake, to adjust to new ideas, to remain vigilant, and to face the challenge of change."

Unfortunately, we live in a time when Dr. King's worries about the church have largely come true. I dare say that the contemporary church can rightly be called protectors of the status quo and fraternities of the indifferent, for people are literally dying at our doorstep, but we are doing nothing about it. Furthermore, we are losing entire generations. We have churches dying in cities though they are surrounded by people on every side. Most young adults today consider the church to be a nonfactor in engaging the critical struggles in times like these. Many consider the church as being more consumed with preserving its history and traditions than fighting for justice and improving the daily lives of people.

Many young people view the church in the same light as another one of the most important voices of the twentieth century, Tupac Amaru Shakur, who called churches "ghetto mansions"—pretty to look at, but doing nothing for their community. Our nation is amid another revolutionary time for racial justice and equality, but it often appears as if the church is asleep at the wheel. For far too many years, as our people were being brutalized by police violence, the church has been silent. For far too many years, as Congress has stripped away the Voting Rights Act, the church has been silent.

For far too many years, as the war on drugs and the prison industrial complex re-enslaved our Black masculinity—and with rapidly increasing numbers, our Black femininity—the church has been silent. Just as problematically, when people begin to speak out for justice today, the church is often the first to criticize and condemn their actions. Just look at the discrepancy in the ways that the church responds to situations of violence in the city of Dallas. Collette Flanagan and her organization, Mothers Against Police Brutality, note that over sixty families in Dallas today are working through her organization to seek answers to the questionable deaths of their loved ones at the hands of Dallas police officers. Until a Black police officer was indicted by a grand jury earlier this month for killing a Latinx youth, it had been over forty years since any police officer had been indicted in the murder of a citizen in Dallas. Over the course of forty years of death and destruction, the church has largely been silent. No, the church has been dormant—asleep.

While there have been nonviolent protests, marches, and demonstrations for years that call attention to this violence, the church has been asleep, hard to find, and failing to speak up and resist. But this past summer, as soon as a lone, deranged gunman tragically opened fire on police after another rally and march in Dallas had ended without incident (people were already going home), suddenly many in the church started to condemn the nonviolent protestors. They asked us, "Why were you out there, anyway?"

Well, let me tell you why we were out there: We were out there because our people are dying daily in the streets for selling CDs, missing a traffic signal, and playing their music too loud. It doesn't matter if we're standing with our hands up or lying on the ground handcuffed—we care. That's why we're out there. And the church should care as much about this violence as any other form of violence. When the church doesn't, it's deeply troubling. And revealing. In times like these, when the church is needed the most, the church is slumbering, and a wake-up call is undeniably in order. It's time for the alarm clock to ring.

In our text, we find evidence of the tragedies that befall us all when the church is asleep. But we also find hope for what happens when the church wakes up. The apostle Paul was preaching in Troas, a seaport city and Roman province in Asia where he had stayed for a week after arriving by ship from Philippi. Because he was leaving the next day, the Bible says that Paul preached all day long, all the way to midnight.

Surely Paul had an important message. And it's undeniable that Paul possessed a sharp theological mind. But in this text, it appears as if neither Paul nor the church gathered around him did well in discerning the time. Even good things done at the wrong time can have fatal consequences. Paul preached so long that candles had to be lit in the upstairs room to provide some light.

The Bible says that a young man named Eutychus was sitting on the windowsill of the third floor. As he sat there, Paul kept going on and on. Eutychus became so drowsy that he fell into a deep sleep. As he slept, Eutychus fell out of the window and plunged to his death, three stories down. It would be easy to condemn Eutychus for his own death.

We could say that he never should have sat on the windowsill. We could say he shouldn't have fallen asleep in church. We could say he has no one to blame but himself. But you can't condemn Eutychus if you don't look at his environment. Here is a young man dwelling on the edge. Here is a young man sitting for hours upon the brink of disaster. Here is a young man perilously close to tragedy. But no one in the church said a word. Not the preacher. Not the ushers. Not the saints gathered there. No one invited him down and made room for him on the floor. And although he was present with them, no one paid enough attention to him to know he was getting sleepy. They only took notice of him after he succumbed to his environment. Too often, the church only takes notice of people who are living on the edge after tragedy befalls them.

This is a great tragedy. Although this young man is the one who fell asleep, I declare that it was the church that needed to stay woke. The church was so consumed with itself that it forgot about those living in danger on the margins. The church was so consumed with itself that it carried on for hours, but never moved the people into action. The church was so consumed with itself that it allowed a young man to die on its watch. As a matter of fact, one Bible scholar states that Eutychus' environment contributed directly to his condition because since the room contained many lamps and people, it stands to reason that oxygen levels were low. They were low enough for everyone present to be a bit light-headed. The lack of oxygen present could have been enough to cause young Eutychus to sit in the window. How many young people today are sitting in the window because a slumbering church is suffocating them?

There is some good news in the text, however, some hope. It's found in Eutychus' name. His name in Greek means "good fortune"—or, we might say, lucky. The Bible says that Paul went down, bent over Eutychus, took him in his arms and told everybody not to worry, for the boy was alive. Then they went up and shared in the Lord's Supper. Paul spoke life into a dead situation, and a dead situation came back to life. This is what happens when the church is woke. But we know that Eutychus was not simply lucky; he was a blessed child of God.

We, too, should be able to declare that despite all the times we have sat on the edge, despite all the times we have been in perilous situations, despite all the fatal situations that we have faced, we are still blessed, for we are still God's children. What was true then is true now: When the church is woke, new life comes to dead situations and overcomes fatal circumstances. When the church is woke, the captives are set free. When the church is woke, signs and wonders follow. When the church is woke, healing and deliverance take place. When the church is woke, the people are not condemned; they are empowered. Church, in times like these, we must wake up! And stay woke!

To Hell with H.U.G.S.!
Ecclesiastes 3:1–5

(Delivered on October 6, 2019, in Dallas, Texas, following
the trial of former Dallas police officer Amber Guyger,
who murdered Botham Jean.)

Fifty-one years ago, during the first week of April 1968, Dr. King began preparing to return to Memphis, Tennessee, to support striking sanitation workers. According to a gentleman named Pastor Graham from Macon, Georgia, whom I met almost fifteen years ago in Atlanta before departing for Memphis, Dr. King had called together several leaders of the movement and instructed them that no matter what was to come in the future, they must endeavor to stay together.

According to friends in Montgomery, Alabama, Dr. King also traveled there, returning to his old neighborhood where he once had lived with his family in the Dexter Avenue Baptist Church parsonage. He briefly visited with old friends and even got a haircut at the local barbershop.

At some time before he departed for Memphis that week on April 3, Dr. King also prepared a sermon to preach at Ebenezer Baptist Church in Atlanta, where he served as co-pastor with his father. The title of the sermon was placed on the church's marquee, and he was off. The next day, while standing on a Memphis motel balcony, he was nearly decapitated by an assassin's bullet.

The title of the sermon that Dr. King completed but never preached was "Why America May Go to Hell." While we are not privy to the manuscript of this sermon, we are privy, in a sense, to Dr. King's inclinations at the time. He was no longer a twenty-six-year-old minister with a newly minted Ph.D. pastoring his first church with his beautiful young wife at his side. He was almost forty, a general and a veteran of the civil rights struggle. He body bore the scars of many attacks, and while still filled with hope, Dr. King's disposition and language had become decidedly more radical in opposition to the evil of white supremacy. He understood more clearly than ever that "freedom is never given voluntarily by the oppressor; it must be demanded by the oppressed."[17]

In his final book, *Where Do We Go from Here: Chaos or Community?*, published in 1967, Dr. King wrote, "Why is equality so assiduously avoided? Why does white America delude itself, and how does it rationalize the evil it retains ... The majority of white America consider themselves sincerely committed to justice for the Negro ... But unfortunately, this is a fantasy of self-deception and comfortable vanity."[18]

Dr. King was arguing that many white Americans are not truly committed to the liberation of Black people. Sometimes, when it appears as if white America is for making racial progress, they are for maintaining their societal status and personal comfort.

Unfortunately, I believe we saw this play out once again across America after a display of uncommon forgiveness in a Dallas courtroom. This week, after his brother's murderer had been found guilty of that crime, during his victim impact statement, eighteen-year-old Brandt Jean spoke directly to Amber Guyger from the stand: "I don't want to say twice or for the one hundredth time what you've or how much you have taken from us. I think you know that. But ... I hope you go to God with all the guilt, all the bad things you have done in the past. If you truly are sorry, I know I can speak for myself, I forgive you. And I know if you go to God and ask him, he will forgive you ... I love you ... Give your life to Christ!"[19]

Then young Brandt asked the judge if he might embrace his brother's killer, and when she granted his request, Brandt Jean came down from the stand and embraced Amber Guyger in the courtroom. Although this young man has been roundly chastised for making this statement and for taking this action, I must go on record and confess that it was one of the greatest individual acts of Christian love and compassion that I have ever witnessed.

If you truly believe in a God who loves all and forgives all who profess their sins to God, you must accept that yes, even Amber Guyger, even in that moment, was welcome to receive the full grace of God; and for that, you ought to give God the praise!

However, not long after I witnessed this tremendous act of Christian love and compassion unfold, I witnessed other things that made my stomach turn. One of our elected officers in the city of Dallas made a Facebook post. That post read: "#LoveYourNeighbor #BeLikeBo #BeLikeBrandt." I found it very offensive because this was the same man who voted against paid sick leave for three hundred twenty thousand of his poorest neighbors in Dallas. This was the same man who opposed removing monuments to white supremacy in Dallas. This was the same man who opposed placing a residential center for the underprivileged in his district. This was the same man who opposed placing new affordable housing in his district. All these things would have helped largely Black and Brown people in this city; but now, he wanted to celebrate a forgiving hug from a Black man to a white woman.

I scrolled down and saw another post, this time from a white pastor. He posted that the hug that happened in the courtroom was not because of Brandt's agency, but rather, because of "thousands of church members praying for the outcome." He went on to say, quoting a former Dallas mayor, that the reason Dallas has not exploded like other cities after injustices is "directly related to the pastors who meet together on a regular basis and speak peace and forgiveness in our faith gatherings out of their trusted friendships with each other." I was furious because I know which pastors he was speaking of. I know they never show up or stand up for anything in this city. I also know the history of this city and that the white business establishment used Black pastors to quell requests for justice during the civil rights movement, and they shut out Dr. King from coming to Dallas.

After Brandt Jean's expression of forgiveness, Amber Guyger's attorney used the hug to appeal for an even lighter sentence for his client, and the Dallas Police Department used the hug to say they wanted to hug it out with the community and simply move forward, forgiving and trusting one another. I saw many other posts celebrating the hug from people who, if the deceased had been their family member, would have requested a front-row seat in the execution chamber. And if the murderer had been Black or Brown, they may have requested to do the execution themselves.

Here was a white official and a white pastor, a white attorney and a police department, and a city not just celebrating a hug, but turning that hug into a weapon of injustice. Their promotion of the hug was to present Dallas as a Christlike city, full of love and compassion for others. It was as if they wanted to place the picture of this hug on a postcard and mail it across the world saying, "Welcome to Dallas."

But I recall another postcard that was made and mailed across the world as a welcome to Dallas. It was not a postcard depicting a hug, but rather a postcard showing the lynching of a Black man named Allen Brooks in downtown Dallas as the city was on its way to building the largest Ku Klux Klan chapter in America.

No, this is not a Christlike city, not when the following is true:

- Dallas is dead last (number 274 of 274 American cities) in racial segregation and racial inequity (Urban Institute).
- Dallas leads the nation in the deportation of our neighbors.
- One half of Dallas residents can't afford their basic needs (United Way).
- The overwhelming majority (70 percent) of Dallas' homeless are Black.
- Black people comprise 20 percent of Dallas residents but 50 percent of all arrests.
- Half of the nation's transgendered female population murdered this year have been murdered here in Texas.
- Texas will be the last state in the nation to raise the age category for youth offenders versus adult offenders (we don't show grace or forgiveness to kids, especially Black and Brown ones).

- Texas has executed more people than any other state.
- Texas houses 10 percent of all hate groups in America.
- Texas still has kids in cages at our border.

I wrote a response to those trying to co-op the moment between Brandt Jean and Amber Guyer:

> Don't you dare hijack #BrandtJean's act of forgiveness and grace as emblematic of who we are or the work we have done. The Jean family has headed back to St. Lucia, but there are dozens of Dallasites still seeking justice for their loved ones murdered by police. And we have failed them.
>
> Brandt Jean's act was a courageous, individual act of Christian forgiveness, not a sign that Dallas has mastered racial reconciliation, grace, forgiveness, or justice. Preachers, we have nothing to pat ourselves on the back for. As Dr. King said, "True peace is not the absence of tension; it's the presence of justice."

Yes, they were quick to post a hug, but I did not see them also post a grieving mother's words. Allison Jean left us with a charge before she returned home: "There is much more to be done in the city of Dallas. The corruption that we saw must stop and it must stop for you who live in Dallas ... Our life must move on, but it must move on with change. There's got to be a better day."

On Friday, as we stood with the Jean family at our church empowerment center, Mrs. Jean said, "Talk but no action means nothing." Dallas should heed the words of the prophet Ezekiel, who said, "They lead my people astray, saying 'Peace,' when there is no peace, and because, when a flimsy wall is built, they cover it with whitewash, therefore tell those who cover it with whitewash that it is going to fall."[20]

This week, we have witnessed two hugs—a hug of compassion and forgiveness, and the weaponizing of the hug to retain evil white supremacy and white comfort. And in this nation, there is a long tradition of white people weaponizing Black forgiveness to escape accountability and to ease their consciousness.

That is why we must understand that all hugs are not equal. Some hugs are not truly hugs. Some hugs are hate undermining genuine sincerity (H.U.G.S.). And to that I say, "To hell with hate undermining genuine sincerity."

The writer of Ecclesiastes lets us know that some hugs are to be rejected. We must be aware of hateful hugs and the hate-filled season in which we live. The writer of Ecclesiastes is concerned about the times in which people live, and, as one Bible scholar notes, the times require an appropriate human action. These times require either constructive action to build things up or destructive action to tear things down.

So, the writer pens in Ecclesiastes 3,

1 For everything there is a season,
  a time for every activity under heaven.

2 A time to be born and a time to die.
  A time to plant and a time to harvest.

3 A time to kill and a time to heal.
  A time to tear down and a time to build up.

4 A time to cry and a time to laugh.
  A time to grieve and a time to dance.

5 A time to scatter stones and a time to gather stones.
  A time to embrace and a time to turn away.

So, in the spirit of Ecclesiastes, I say, to hell with H.U.G.S. We will not be quelled! We will not be silent! We will not be pacified! We will not be stopped! We will not stop fighting for justice until justice flows like waters, and righteousness like a mighty stream!

You Gonna Learn Today!
Luke 10:25–37

(Delivered January 12, 2017, in Los Angeles, California,
as the revivalist for the Theology in the Hood Conference.)

The first full week in the presidency of Donald J. Trump was both harrowing and horrifying. This, unfortunately, comes as no surprise to anyone who has followed his rhetoric and practices—not just during the recent presidential campaign, not just during the Obama administration, but for decades earlier. This past week, it appeared as if President Trump was in a race against himself to see how much damage he could cause to American democracy and to our global stability.

In one week, with the stroke of a pen, President Trump suspended a planned cut to interest rates by the Department of Housing and Urban Development, making it harder for Americans to purchase a home. He instructed agencies to waive or grant exceptions to the Affordable Care Act and canceled advertisements encouraging people to sign up for healthcare, thus ensuring that millions will be dropped from coverage due to age and pre-existing conditions, and that people with life-threatening conditions may no longer be able to afford life-saving treatments.

He signed support of the Keystone XL Pipeline, which had been rejected for years because of environmental concerns, and he signed support to the Dakota Access Pipeline, which if constructed will threaten the water supply and overall ecology of sacred tribal lands. It is important to note that this proposed pipeline was rerouted through tribal lands because of concerns that it might threaten the water supply and overall ecology of a majority-white community.

He placed a freeze on hiring in the federal government, leaving thousands of jobs unfilled, including at the Department of Veteran Affairs. That means five hundred thousand people who have made tremendous sacrifices for the security of our nation will continue to wait for a month, on average, to be seen at the VA. He instructed the Department of Homeland Security to begin building a wall between the United States and Mexico, and he expanded current immigration laws so that a person given a ticket for driving without a license can be placed on the accelerated deportation list for committing an act "that constitutes a chargeable criminal offense."

Within days of his administration taking office, President Trump signed an executive order blocking immigrants and visa holders from seven majority-Muslim countries: Iraq, Iran, Syria, Libya, Yemen, Somalia, and the Sudan. The order also blocks the entry of people from these countries who are green card holders or permanent US residents. Furthermore, he suspended the US refugee program for one hundred twenty days and the Syrian refugee administration program indefinitely, though our world is facing the worse refugee crisis in world history. There presently are more people displaced from their homes now than during World War II.

There are reports that President Trump is preparing to make more moves quickly. It is reported that he wants to cut federal funding to public broadcasting, which includes *Sesame Street* and *PBS Newshour*, the most unbiased news source in America, and he wanted to close the Civil Rights Division of the Department of Justice. This just one month after President Obama signed the Emmett Till Bill to reopen civil rights-era cases before 1970 and seek justice for murders and acts of terror for which no justice has been rendered. He does this as Carolyn Bryant Donham, eighty-two, now admits that she fabricated the story of sexual assault that led her former husband and his half brother to torture, shoot, and throw young Till's body in a Mississippi river nearly sixty-two years earlier.

It is particularly unfortunate that President Trump wants to cut public broadcasting. Thirty years ago, public broadcasting helped my generation learn who our neighbors were. Each day,

Mr. Rogers' Neighborhood would broadcast on my television screen, and Mr. Fred Rogers inquired in song what I believe now to have been a profound question: "Who are the people in your neighborhood, in your neighborhood, in your neighborhood? Who are the people in your neighborhood?" He's ultimate response was "it's the people that you meet each day."

For my children's generation, it is a different show: *Daniel Tiger's Neighborhood*. But the emphasis is the same—we are all neighbors. We are neighbors, not just in the sense that we live in close proximity to one another, but in the greater sense that we share this world, and in so doing, as Dr. Martin Luther King Jr. so eloquently stated, "we must all learn to live together as brothers or we will all perish together as fools. We are tied together in the single garment of destiny, caught in an inescapable network of mutuality. And whatever affects one directly affects all indirectly ... I can never be what I ought to be until you are what you ought to be. That is the way God's universe is made, this is the way it is structured."[21]

Yes, I believe that President Trump and millions of others who share his views do not know who their neighbors are; for if you knew your neighbors, you would not cut their healthcare; you would not separate their families; you would not spread lies about them; you would not poison their drinking water; and you surely would not leave them and their families detained for hours at our nation's airports simply because they practice a faith different from your own.

Still, this is not the first time we have encountered an issue of not knowing or celebrating our neighbors. This is an issue as old as antiquity. This is an issue frozen in time through scripture. This is an issue that Jesus himself addressed, for knowing our neighbor is critical to the health and survival of our world.

In the text, one day a religious scholar approached Jesus to test him or to trick him concerning his knowledge of religious law. He asked Jesus, "Rabbi, what should I do to inherit eternal life?" Jesus inquired, "What does the law of Moses say? How do you read it?" And the man said, "'You must love the Lord your God with all your heart, all your soul, all your strength, and all your mind.' And 'Love your neighbor as yourself.'" To this, Jesus responded,

"Right! Do this and you will live!"

Now clearly, the conversation could have ended here. Jesus expertly answered the man's question according to religious law. Nothing more needed to be said. There was nothing that could be misunderstood. But the religious expert was not satisfied with the truth because he was not looking for the truth. No, he was looking to trap. Please understand that in this post-truth, alternative-facts era in which we live, not everyone who approaches you in real life or on social media is interested in the truth. They may be looking to trap you instead!

The Bible says, "The man wanted to justify his actions, so he asked Jesus, 'And who is my neighbor?'" And in my spiritual imagination, I see Jesus saying to himself, "Oh, you want to go there? Well, class is now in session. You gonna learn today!"

Then Jesus began to tell a story: "A Jewish man was traveling from Jerusalem down to Jericho, and he was attacked by bandits. They stripped him of his clothes, beat him up, and left him half dead beside the road. By chance a priest came along. But when he saw the man lying there, he crossed to the other side of the road and passed him by. A temple assistant walked over and looked at him lying there, but he also passed by on the other side."

Here, my friends, Jesus reveals a necessary truth: Not everyone who goes to church or speaks from the church's lexicon is the church. That is, our faith without works is dead, and some people are more committed to talking the talk rather than walking the walk. The man who is left for dead on the side of the road is a human being, a neighbor, someone who well could have been a member of their congregation.

Why did they leave him for dead? I am sure that they left him because they were afraid that if they helped their neighbor after he had suffered so greatly, the people who attacked him might come back and attack them as well. And friends, this is true. When you stand up for justice, when you walk with the marginalized and oppressed, the same people who threaten and oppose them may threaten and oppose you as well.

But then the Bible says that "a despised Samaritan came along, and when he saw the man, he felt compassion for him. The Samaritan soothed his wounds with olive oil and wine and bandaged them. Then he put the man on his own donkey and took him to an inn, where he took care of him. [And] the next day, he handed the innkeeper two silver coins [and told him] 'Take care of this man. If his bill runs higher than this, I'll pay you the next time I'm here.'"

The amazing thing in the text is that Jews and Samaritans were not supposed to get along. They had different centers of worship. They had negative history dating back to Jewish reentry into the promised land after their exile. They were practically cousins, but their mutual hatred ran deep. They had no dealing with each other. And yet, it was the Samaritan who took care of the Jew.

The Samaritan refused to allow history, a different approach to faith, or what present society dictated about the other man to stop him from treating the Jew with love and human dignity. Jesus then asked the religious expert, "Now which of these three would you say was a neighbor to the man who was attacked by bandits?" And the man replied, "The one who showed him mercy." Then Jesus said, "Yes, now go and do the same."

There is a greater revelation of importance in the text. In 63 B.C., Samaria was annexed with the Roman province of Syria. Samaria and Syria are the same. That means in their time of need, we are banning from this nation the descendants of the man Jesus illuminated to teach us all to be good neighbors. We are banning good neighbors by refusing to be good neighbors.

Oh, but I declare that we gonna learn today! We are going to learn to stand up against injustice, for injustice anywhere is a threat to justice everywhere! We are going to learn to love our neighbors as ourselves. We are going to learn that if God be for us, who can be against us! We are going to learn to stand together, pray together, march together, rally together, vote together, resist together, side by side, neighbor to neighbor, until justice flows like waters and righteousness like a mighty stream.

We are going to learn, in the words of Hezekiah Walker, that we need one another to survive the harms of this present age so we can build together a greater and more equitable future. We are going to learn, in the words of the Apostle Paul, that "the body is a unit, though it is made up of many parts; and though all its parts are many, they form one body. So, it is with Christ."[22] We are going to learn in the words of that historic chant for justice that "the people, united, can never be defeated!"

And when our enemies seek to divide and oppress us, they are going to learn today that no weapon formed against us shall prosper, for we are more than conquerors in Christ Jesus![23]

The Valley
Ezekiel 37:1–3

(Delivered September 9, 2018, in Wichita, Kansas,
for the ReVOTElution Wichita Voter Awareness Project.)

Early one Friday morning, I was contacted by my friend and brother John Fullinwider, a longtime activist in Dallas with whom I have worked with on many justice matters. He is one of the co-founders of Mothers Against Police Brutality. John texted me a flyer accompanied by an inquiry: "Can you come and say a few words?"

The flyer pictured a handsome, young Black man, whom I would later learn was an immigrant to America from the Eastern Caribbean island of St. Lucia. He had come to America to matriculate at Harding University, a private liberal arts college in Arkansas, where he excelled academically and was a student leader. He was a Christian who actively shared his faith as a Bible study leader at his church in West Dallas, and as a worship leader with his beautiful singing voice, which he used to usher all who heard him into the awesome presence of God.

I knew the mere fact that John was contacting me about him meant the young man was dead. I knew the mere fact that John was contacting me about him meant that he likely was killed by the police. Over the last several years, I frequently have been called upon to memorialize beautiful Black people killed at the hands of police. I have been called to speak at vigils, at rallies, at protests, and at press conferences. I also have memorialized the fallen with my pen, and those memorials have been published and shared around the world. I have sat for my fair share of interviews beamed across the globe for the same. Despite this, I have never allowed these incidents to become normalized for me. With each new tragedy, whether local or national, I have been horrified anew.

Yes, I knew that the young man on the flyer was dead, but why? What I learned still does not make sense. On Thursday night, this young man was at his flat in the upwardly mobile Cedars community of Dallas, immediately adjacent to downtown from the south. I learned that someone was attempting to enter his flat. I learned that he went to the door to see who was attempting to enter his home. When he got to the door, he discovered a police officer seeking to gain entrance into his home. When he opened the door, the police officer shot him through the heart.

So, we gathered in front of the Dallas Police headquarters on Friday evening under cloudy skies, a heavy rain having turned into a light drizzle. It is a place we have frequented over the years as other persons have been killed. I was handed the megaphone to speak, and with the crowd that had gathered, I began to share something else that I had learned: the meaning of the deceased's name. I have long been fascinated by the etymology of names, and the victim had a unique name which begged to be explored.

His name is Botham Jean. Say his name. Say his name. Say his name.

I learned that his name means "he who lives in a broad valley." I told the crowd that I felt that "a broad valley" was a useful descriptor of the pains of police brutality and injustices that we face in our nation. For our faith, the valley has served as a metaphor for a season of lament, a place of great sorrow and despair. And ofttimes in America, it feels as if we are walking through a broad valley, one senseless tragedy falling upon the heels of another, piling up upon itself.

The valley reeks of death and destruction. Did not the psalmist say, "Yea, though I walk through the valley of the shadow of death"? Countless battles and bloodshed in the Bible happen in the valley. But a broad valley speaks to a place that it is not easy to depart from.

Have you ever felt like you were in a broad valley? Have you ever been in a season when one tragedy begat another tragedy, which begat yet another? Have you ever been moved to tears by the moaning and groanings of our society? Does it disturb you that fifty years after the Kerner Commission Report, wealth disparity in America has increased? Does it disturb you that it would take 228 years for the median wealth of a Black family to equal the same for a white family in America? Are you grieved to learn that nearly sixty-five years after *Brown* v. *Board of Education*, two hours away in Topeka and sixty years after the Dockum Drug Store sit-ins here in Wichita—one of the first organized sit-ins in the United States—our society is rapidly resegregating itself?

Are you troubled when you hear of another mass shooting, from bullets unleashed in a Bible study to shots ringing out in schools? Are you troubled to see white supremacists march through the streets with torches, or when the president calls them good people, but refers to Black female leadership as ignorant and dogs, and calls Black professional athletes SOBs and Black-controlled nations S-hole countries?

Are you troubled when you hear that the police are called on Black people for the crime of existing, for the crime of barbequing in a park, for being a student asleep in your dormitory, for waiting for a business associate for coffee at Starbucks, for mowing a lawn, and on, and on, and on? Yes, sometimes it feels like we are walking through a broad valley.

I can only imagine what it must have felt like for the prophet Ezekiel when the LORD carried him into the valley. The Bible does not tell us exactly which valley Ezekiel was carried to, but it does tell us what was awaiting him when he arrived. It was a horrific scene. Everywhere Ezekiel looked, he saw evidence of mass causalities and trauma. The entire valley floor was covered with human remains. He could not move without stumbling over a bone. His was the scene of an army who had lost a major battle with no survivors present to bury the dead.

And not only was the valley floor covered in bones, but they were also dry bones. This means the death and destruction present in the valley was not a new reality; but rather, it had been present for some time. Now, I don't know about you, but sometimes I like to push back on the text. It would appear to me to be rather cruel for God to bring Ezekiel to a place of such pain and horror and to just drop him off there. Why would God force Ezekiel to be present amid such tragedy? Maybe it's because God always needs a witness, and to be a witness for God sometimes means that you must be present in troubling spaces.

And it is here, while surrounded by bones, that God poses a question to Ezekiel: "Son of man, can these bones become living people again?" Take special note when God asks someone a question. God is all-knowing, all-present, all-powerful. Therefore, God never asks a question for information. God asks questions for our revelation, to reveal to us the deeper meanings of the Spirit of God.

I like Ezekiel's response. Yes, Ezekiel is a prophet of God. Yes, he has accomplished mighty exploits for the Kingdom of God. But Ezekiel does not feel the need to act like he knows things he does not. He is not compelled to add a lot of church talk and spiritual highlights to this tragedy to cover for his insecurity or to insulate him from what surrounds him. No, he simply says, "O Sovereign LORD, you alone know that." Essentially, Ezekiel says, "I don't know, but if there is anyone who can know, it would be you because you are sovereign, God, you are the supreme ruler, you possess the ultimate power.

Somebody missed their shout. Ezekiel is saying, yes, I am in the valley. Yes, I am surrounded by heartache and tragedy. Yes, there is death and destruction on every hand. But even here in the valley, you are still in charge. Isn't that good news? God is not only the God of the mountaintop; God is the God of the valley. Is there anybody that can testify that even amid the valley, I am not left to my own defenses? "Yea, though I walk through the valley of the shadow of death, I will fear no evil, for you are with me. Your rod and staff, they comfort me."

This is the hope of the valley! No matter how dark things may seem, no matter the troubles on every hand, God is with me!

Then God told Ezekiel, "Speak a prophetic word to these bones. Say dry bones, listen to the word of the LORD." Don't miss the imperative in this text. No matter what is going on in our world, no matter the tragedy that confronts us, we cannot turn away from it, but we must speak out. For every injustice, for every tragedy, for every abuse, there is a Word from the LORD, and we must be God's representative even in the valley!

When Ezekiel spoke, there was a rattling in the valley, and scattered bones began to reconnect as if drawn together by a magnetic force. As Ezekiel looked out, scattered bones were now gathered bones as skeletons were formed. Then muscles and skin formed over the bones. But even still, Ezekiel was surrounded by corpses. So, the LORD said, "Speak to the winds."

Don't miss it! First, God had Ezekiel speak to the bones, to the trauma, to the despair, to the destruction. Now, God had Ezekiel speak beyond the bones, beyond the trauma, beyond the despair, and beyond the destruction, and speak to the Spirit. In scripture, the Spirit often is identified by the wind. And when the Spirit shows up, tragedy is turned into triumph, defeat is turned to dignity, pain is turned to power. For I am reminded of the words of the Christ as he read from the scroll:

The Spirit of the LORD *is* upon Me,
Because He has anointed Me
To preach the gospel to *the* poor;
He has sent Me to heal the brokenhearted,
To proclaim liberty to *the* captives
And recovery of sight to *the* blind,
To set at liberty those who are oppressed;
To proclaim the acceptable year of the LORD.[24]

And as Ezekiel spoke, new life came into a dead situation, and the corpses stood as a mighty army.

Yes, there are troubles on every side. Yes, it seems like we are walking through a broad valley, but there is still hope in the valley, for the people of God are a people of hope.

I declare that there is joy in the valley!
I declare that there is peace in the valley!
I declare that there is hope in the valley!
I declare that there is deliverance in the valley!
I declare that there is love in the valley!
I declare that there is truth in the valley!

The Spirit of the LORD is in the valley, and "where the Spirit of the LORD is, there is liberty!"[25]

Where Do We Go from Here?
Numbers 13:25-30

(Delivered September 8, 2019, in Omaha, Nebraska, as a featured speaker for community events leading to the centennial commemoration of the Red Summer of 1919 and the lynching of Will Brown.)

There is an image of the Reverend Dr. Martin Luther King Jr. that is rarely seen or remembered. It was taken not in the American South but rather in the city of Chicago on August 5, 1966, as Dr. King was helping to lead a march in Marquette Park.[26]

This is the same city where, in January, three officers were acquitted of cover-up in the brutal murder of seventeen-year-old Laquan McDonald, who was shot sixteen times by Officer Jason Van Dyke—even though the officer's reports contradicted the actual video of the shooting, including the false claim that McDonald had attempted to harm the officers.

Laquan McDonald—say his name. Say his name. Say his name.

The picture is misleading when viewed out of context. At first, it might appear that there are people attacking Dr. King. However, the white and Black men flanking Dr. King in the picture did not mean him any harm. In fact, they were protecting him, shielding him from any further injury. That August of 1966, a mob of nearly seven hundred also had come to the park, hurling stones at Dr. King from every direction. One stone had struck Dr. King, knocking him to his knees, where he remained until his equilibrium returned.

To be clear, Dr. King was being stoned for the crimes of seeking fair and affordable housing, a living wage, and strong, well-funded schools for Black people in Chicago. In 1966, Chicago held the highest per capita income of any city in the world. Yet, most residents in the Black community of Chicago did not benefit from this prosperity. Dr. King once called the Black ghettos of Chicago "an island of poverty in the midst of an ocean of plenty." He also noted that the hate and hostility that he experienced in Chicago were greater than any he had seen or experienced in the South.

It is exceedingly important that we remember this image of Dr. King—not the Martin King of many contemporary fantasies, not even the King who marched triumphantly into Washington and Montgomery, who was adorned with the Nobel Peace Prize in Oslo, and who was adored by overflow audiences. We must remember *this* King—hated and reviled by millions both Black and white, wiretapped and hunted by the FBI, betrayed by former justice colleagues, and less than two years from having his head nearly severed by an assassin's bullet on a Memphis balcony.

We must remember this King, whose name and movement had a disapproval rating near 70 percent at the time of his death, because this is the King who penned his final book, *Where Do We Go from Here: Chaos or Community?*, which was first published in 1967. In a foreword in a later edition, Coretta Scott King, a faithful freedom fighter in the Black liberation struggle and Dr. King's widow, , hoped that the book would be viewed as his last will and testament, outlining not only the great trials and tribulations that remained for our nation and our world, but also proposing detailed solutions for the same.

Unfortunately, today we live in an era where the words and image of Dr. King have been largely co-opted by forces opposed to his radical vision of justice. His witness and words, which inspired people to live lives of self-sacrifice for the liberation of their neighbors, are now used instead to quell quests for justice and to sell trucks during the Super Bowl. In many ways, Dr. King has been transformed into a sort of jolly Black Santa Claus, bearing gifts of peace and love, not the radical revolutionary who fought valiantly in the face of great odds. Like ventriloquists, we have made Dr. King's deadened mouth utter what another man named King uttered—"Can't we all just get along?"[27]—instead of the words he actually spoke, like "freedom is never voluntarily given by the oppressor; it must be demanded by the oppressed."

Let me tell you what failing to remember the true and radical King and the movement that he helped to lead has wrought. Fifty years after his death, the legacy of redlining and unfair housing remains, and there are fewer Black homeowners today than in 1968. Incarceration rates have increased with the War on Drugs, the laws of which were purposely designed to ensnare Black, Brown, and poor bodies. Laws are now changing only because of an opioid crisis among whites, while thousands of Black and Brown people remain incarcerated for selling drugs— many of which are now legal—drugs that are earning (primarily) white people outrageous profits in many states.

A recent Yale University study revealed preschool teachers spend more time watching little Black boys, expecting trouble, than any other student. Our public schools have been virtually resegregated since 1988. Black unemployment remains nearly twice as high as for other racial groups. In fact, economists report that there is such a massive racial wealth disparity in America that it would take 228 years for median Black family wealth to equate to that of median white family wealth. And Black women, the most highly educated demographic in America[28], would have to work an additional 233 days in a year to earn what a white man earns in a year.

It now appears that ninety years after his birth and fifty years since his brutal death, when Dr. King poetically and prophetically inquired, "Where do we go from here?", America has responded, "Nowhere. Here is good enough."

Truthfully, King may have foreseen this response; for he wrote, "White America was ready to demand that the Negro should be spared the lash of brutality and coarse degradation, but it had never been truly committed to helping him out of poverty, exploitation, or all forms of discrimination."

America now appears stuck—stuck between the heroic sacrifices of her past and the hopeful promise of her just future. America seems stuck, circling a mountain in a desert of despair.

America's "stuckness" on the precipice of true yet unrealized greatness reminds me of another nation stuck in the same.

It was at Kadesh, in the wilderness of the Paran desert, that Moses, Aaron, and the whole community of Israel were first confronted with the question "where do we go from here?" For forty days, scouts from Israel had surveyed the land of Canaan with instructions from Moses to "see what the land was like, to find out whether the people living there were weak or strong, few or many. [To] see what kind of land they live in, whether their towns had walls, whether the soil was fertile or poor, to count the trees, and to bring back samples of the crops."[29]

When the scouts returned, they declared, "We entered the land you sent us to explore, and it is indeed a bountiful country—a land flowing with milk and honey ... But the people living there are powerful, and their towns are large and fortified ... We can't go up against them. They are stronger than we are!"[30]

And maybe this is what has our nation stuck as well. Yes, we see the promise—the promise of a world and nation void of racism, bigotry, discrimination, hate, yes, even white supremacy—but we are aware that laying claim to this new reality will require that we fully face and defeat these opposing giants once and for all.

A mighty inquiry arose in the Paran desert that day. Where do we go from here?

And the majority, responding with fear and uncertainty, whined, "Let's stay right here." Later, other voices even proposed returning to Egypt, to the pain of their past, the very place of their bondage.

But a man named Caleb from the Tribe of Judah—whose name means "faithful, devoted, bold, and brave"—proclaimed, "Let's go at once to take the land. We can certainly conquer it!" To the question of "where do we go from here?", Caleb's response was clear: "We go to the promised land!"

What inspired Caleb to want to go to the promised land? My friend Rabbi Andrew Paley of Temple Shalom in Dallas informs me that the command to remember is the most repeated command in the Torah. The command to remember appears thirty-six times in the Torah. The command to remember is specifically the command to remember how God brought Israel out of bondage in Egypt to lead them into the promised land.

Hence, Caleb dared to remember what God had already done for his people, and Caleb dared to believe that God had the power to do it again. If God led us out of slavery, God can do it again! If God brought us out of oppression, God can do it again! If God brought us out of Jim Crow, God can do it again!

As the great James Weldon Johnson penned, "We have come over a way that with tears has been watered, we have come, treading our path through the blood of the slaughtered."[31] Yes, if God did it before, God can do it again!

In Dr. King's final speech, delivered at the Mason Temple (Church of God in Christ headquarters) on April 3, 1968, in Memphis, Tennessee, Dr. King proclaimed, "I've been to the mountaintop ... I've seen the promised land. I may not get there with you. But I want you to know tonight, that we, as a people, will get to the promised land!"

And I believe this morning that there are some Calebs and Dr. Kings here today—faithful, devoted, bold, and brave—who, in the face of the giants who still stand before us, will choose to remember the true and radical Dr. King, and who will choose to remember the power of our God to boldly lead our nation into the promised land.

Where are the Calebs who will dare to believe as Dr. King did that "the arc of the moral universe is long, but it bends toward justice"?

Where are the Calebs who will dare to believe as Dr. King did that "one day this nation will rise up and live out the true meaning of its creed: We hold these truths to be self-evident that all men are created equal"?

Where are the Calebs who will dare to believe as Dr. King did that "injustice anywhere is a threat to justice everywhere"?

Where are the Calebs who will dare to believe as Dr. King did that "darkness cannot drive out darkness, only light can do that. Hate cannot drive out hate, only love can do that"?

Then rise, Caleb, arise!
Where do we go from here?
We are going to the promised land!
Glory! Hallelujah! Glory! Hallelujah! Glory! Hallelujah!
We are going to the promised land!

Show Up!
Matthew 1:23

(Delivered October 13, 2019, in Philadelphia, Pennsylvania, during Sunday morning worship at Mother Bethel AME Church.)

On the morning of Saturday, August 3, 2019, a twenty-one-year-old white supremacist from Allen, Texas—a wealthy suburb of Dallas that boasts a 60 million-dollar high school football stadium that, with a capacity of eighteen thousand seats, is the largest home stadium in the state for a single team—drove six hundred fifty miles west to El Paso, Texas. When he arrived at El Paso—an American city that shares a border with Juarez, Mexico, and that is 80-percent Latinx and has been repeatedly listed among America's safest cities—he exited I-10, walked into a Walmart store where many parents were shopping for school supplies with their children, and, using an AK-47, an instrument of war, shot forty-six people, killing twenty-two of them.

May I ask twenty-two of you to stand and to remain standing, if you are able?

This mass shooting is the deadliest mass shooting in America in 2019, the seventh-deadliest since 1949, and the third-deadliest in Texas history. But it is only one of 331 mass shootings in America this year. In fact, thus far in 2019, there have been more mass shootings than days in America. Today is just day 286.

Less than twenty-four hours after the shooting on August 3 in El Paso, twenty-seven people were shot and nine killed in Dayton, Ohio. May I ask nine of you to stand and to remain standing? And on the final Saturday of August, twenty-four people were shot and seven people killed in Odessa and Midland, Texas. May I ask seven more of you to stand and to remain standing if you are able?

Look around.

These who are standing represent the dead in just three mass shootings this year. May God bless the dead.

Please be seated.

In his twenty-three hundred-word manifesto titled "The Inconvenient Truth," which he posted online a mere nineteen minutes before the El Paso massacre began, the domestic terrorist noted that he was motivated to stop the "Hispanic invasion of Texas," uplifting the white supremacist theory of "the Great Replacement." That concept echoed two years earlier on the streets of Charlottesville, Virginia, where largely young, white men marched through those streets with torches, chanting, "You will not replace us!" The El Paso shooter wrote, "If we can get rid of enough people, then our way of life can be more sustainable."

Among the people he got rid of were Jordan and Andre Anchondo. The Anchondos had just dropped off their five-year-old daughter at cheerleader practice and had come to Walmart with their two-month-old son so they could do some school shopping. As the shooting began, Jordan shielded her baby and Andre shielded his wife. The baby was later recovered alive under his dead father and mother, suffering broken fingers, and covered in their blood.

Another person the shooter murdered was Margie Reckard. Margie was the sixty-three-year-old wife of Antonio Basco. Margie had gone to Walmart to do some routine grocery shopping. In the aftermath of the shooting, Antonio not only had to contend with his tragic loss, but also with the idea that no one would be present to mourn and remember Margie's life, as they had few other family members to speak of. Word of Antonio's concern spread like wildfire throughout El Paso and over all forms of media. It spread so widely that on the Friday of Margie's funeral, over seven hundred people filled a church with a seating capacity of five hundred, while another fifteen hundred people stood outside.

People showed up for Margie's funeral, some traveling there from across the country. Over nine hundred floral arrangements showed up from around the world. So many people showed up that the funeral home had to find a larger venue, and still they could not fit all of them in the church. But the people who could not get in did not leave. They simply formed a human circle of presence and prayer around the entire block on which the church sits.

We cannot predict the future. Life is filled with twists and turns. There are mountain highs and there are valley lows. There are days when sunshine floods our windowpanes and there are days when torrential rain clouds cover our skies. Still, no matter what life presents, and no matter what season of life we find ourselves in, we can show up for one another. We can be present for one another.

The same week of Margie's funeral, *The Late Show* host Stephen Colbert was interviewed by CNN's Anderson Cooper. During that interview, Colbert claimed that tragedy is a gift, for it teaches you how to be more fully human. In Colbert's words, we find echoes of Dr. King words that that suffering can be redemptive. Not that suffering should be desired or aspired to, but if rightly appropriated, suffering can shape you and your human witness in powerful ways.

What we witnessed in El Paso following that great tragedy was the ministry of presence. People showed up with their gifts. People showed up with their bodies. People showed up with their prayers. The ministry of presence is one of the most vital ministries that we have in the church. It has been called incarnational ministry, where we embody the mission of Jesus Christ to be present with the troubled, the hurting, the afflicted, the challenged, and the dying.

It is, in fact, the character of God to show up, and this character is often best exemplified in name. There are many important names for God that we find in scripture. There is El Shaddai, which means "God Almighty," "the all-sufficient God," or "the mighty-breasted One." It is a name that illuminates God's strength, God's majesty, God's power when God shows up. One place that we find this name used is in Psalm 91:1: "He who dwells in the shelter of the Most High will abide in the shadow of the Almighty."

There is El Roi, which means, "the God who sees me." After Hagar fled with her child into the wilderness expecting to die, an angel of the LORD appeared to her, and she declared in 16:13, "You are El Roi. You are God who sees me!" When God shows up, God sees the condition that we are in, and if God can see us, then God can see about us!

There is even Yahweh Yireh, or "the God Who provides." When Abraham went up the mountain to sacrifice his son, he declared, "God, God's self will provide a lamb," and instead of sacrificing his son, he found a ram caught in the brush. God will provide!

But my favorite name for God is found in both the Hebrew Bible and in New Testament scripture: Emmanuel, meaning "God who is with us," or, stated another way, "the God who showed up!" It is the name given to Joseph by God through an angel of the LORD who appeared to Joseph in a dream. The angel of the LORD said, "Do not be afraid to take Mary as your wife. For the child within her was conceived by the Holy Spirit ... All of this occurred to fulfill the LORD's message through his prophet, 'Look! The virgin will conceive a child! She will give birth to a son, and they will call him Immanuel, which means 'God is with us.'"[32]

When Jesus showed up, Jesus showed up with power and resources. When Jesus showed up, Jesus showed up with his body. When Jesus showed up, Jesus showed up with his prayers.

No, Jesus did not just send thoughts and prayers. Jesus showed up with resources to make a difference, his body to make a witness, and his prayers to amplify our trust in God. And if we want to be like Jesus, we cannot sit on the sidelines amid trial and tragedy. We, too, must show up with resources to make a difference, our bodies to make a witness, and our prayers to amplify trust in God.

Yes, it is the character of God to show up. But it is the call of God for us to show up as well.

Early on September 6, 2019, I left Dallas and headed to El Paso. That Friday morning, I was invited to attend a rare in-district field hearing of the United States House of Representatives Judiciary Committee's Subcommittee on Immigration and Citizenship titled "Oversight of the Trump Administration's Border Policies and the Relationship Between Anti-Immigrant Rhetoric and Domestic Terrorism." While in attendance, I was able to speak personally to Congresspersons Veronica Escobar, Sheila Jackson Lee, and Jerry Nadler, who chairs that judiciary committee.

I then stood to bear witness at a protest at an American detention center where families have been separated. While there I was invited to offer a prayer of liberation and benediction. I also interviewed with local media regarding this moment in our nation's history.

But ultimately, I showed up at the memorial where those twenty-two lives were stolen, where I had been invited to speak for a rally that evening. As I paid my respects, I saw a man quite frail in his frame kneeling on the ground, tending to flowers at one of the many crosses erected to the deceased. And as I came closer, I recognized the man as Antonio, who was tending his wife's memorial.

I approached him and acknowledged that I had seen him in various media reports. There were tears already in his eyes, but when I approached him wearing my clergy collar, they began to pour more freely. And before I could utter another word, he buried his head in my chest and repeated, again and again, "I feel so alone. I don't know what to do."

And I just held him. Then I prayed and I asked God to comfort him. I asked God to strengthen him. I asked God to give him peace. I asked God to be present with him. I asked God to show up in his life.

But friends, as I was praying to God, I felt God speaking back to me: "No, Michael, you show up. You show up and bring comfort. You show up and demand justice. You show up and work for peace."

Yes, I am grateful that Jesus showed up! He showed up in a feeding trough wrapped in rags. He showed up in a temple as a youth and confounded the priests. He showed up again at a temple, unrolled the scroll of Isaiah, and declared, "The Spirit of the LORD is upon me for He has anointed me to preach good news to the poor, recovery of sight to the blind, release to the captive, to let the oppressed go free, to declare the year of the LORD's favor!"[33]

He showed up on the lakeshore and called to disciples to become fishers of people. He showed up at the pool of Bethesda and a lame man was able to walk. He showed up among the people and a woman with a twelve-year hemorrhage was healed by the hem of his garment. And yes, on Friday morning, he showed up on Calvary's mountain, where he died for all our sins. But early Sunday morning, he showed up resurrected and with all power in his hands. And when he ascended into heaven, he gave gifts to his church so that we too can show up!

We must show up like Aaron and Hur did for Moses and hold up weary arms so that we have victory in the valley. We must show up like Ruth showed up for Naomi and declared, "Wherever you go, I will go; wherever you live, I will live. Your people will be my people, and your God will be my God!" We must show up like Jonathan did for David, protecting him from a mad and murderous administration.

We must show up in season and out of season. Show up for the widow! Show up for the orphan! Show up for the immigrant! Show up for the mass incarcerated! Show up for the victim of gun violence! Show up for the victim of domestic violence! Show up for the racially profiled! Show up for the victim of police brutality!

Show up at the prison! Show up at the hospital! Show up at the school board meeting! Show up at city hall! Show up for the union worker! Show up at the march! Show up at the rally!

Show up for the voiceless! Show up for the homeless! Show up for the working poor!

Show up, for weeping may endure for a night, but joy comes in the morning.[34]

Show up, for the arc of the moral universe is long, but it bends toward justice—but only if you bend it.

Show up, for if God be for you, who can stand against you? Show up!

If you are willing to show up for others, to comfort them in their mourning, to work for their liberation, to stand against their oppression, give God the glory!

Let's continue to work together, stand together, fight together, pray together, build together, and show up, until justice flows like waters, and righteousness like a might stream!

How Much Is Malcolm X's Legacy Worth to You?

(Delivered April 14, 2018, in New York City, New York, as
a featured speaker for "Reclaiming Malcolm X's Legacy,"
a dinner and benefit for the Malcolm X and
Dr. Betty Shabazz Memorial and Educational Center.)

To God be the glory for the things that God has done.

Last week, I had the honor of guiding faith leaders from
many faiths on a pilgrimage through the Deep South to visit
cities significant to the American civil rights movement. I have
led this experience several times before, but not with a group of
colleagues in faith and justice or with my entire family.

Over the course of several days, we entered many tragic and
brutal spaces. We stood together under the carport in Jackson,
Mississippi, where a cowardly assassin shot Medgar Evers in the
back, a space where the concrete is still stained with his blood.

We stood together in the former cotton gin in Glendora,
Mississippi, where fourteen-year-old Emmett Till was tortured
and killed by a group of men—including Black men who were
forced to participate under the threat of death—before being
tossed into the water tied to a gin by barbed wire.

We stood together before the balcony at the former Lorraine
Motel in Memphis where Dr. King's head was nearly severed by
an assassin's bullet fifty years ago.

We stood together in Sixteenth Street Baptist Church in
Birmingham, where four beautiful girls were bombed into
eternity.

We marched together across the Edmund Pettus Bridge in
Selma, Alabama, where men, women, and children were beaten
back with cattle prods, horsewhips, tear gas, and rods ... where
they were stomped under horse hooves, their skulls and ribs
being cracked in the wake.

Yes, it was a painful and necessary journey of remembrance, but it was also a journey of resistance. And this resistance came from the most unlikely of sources—five children who transformed these brutal spaces into vibrant places with their unquenchable joy.

These children, our children, played together in the bedroom of Medgar's home. After a long day of travel, they napped peacefully in that cotton gin. They climbed up and down the hill in front of that Memphis hotel. They climbed trees in the park in the shadows of Sixteenth Street Baptist Church. In Montgomery, they placed their hands into a crater generated by a bomb. They sang joyfully as we crossed the bridge where civil rights icon John Lewis was brutally beaten by a white supremacist.

In many ways, they modeled for us that which is our responsibility: to transform brutal, harrowing spaces into vibrant places, to hew out joy from great sorrow, yes, to remember, but also to boldly proclaim the promise and hope of a better day.

However, there is one great concern that arose from our travels. Many great men and women along the pilgrimage were honored and celebrated for their great sacrifices for the benefit of all humanity. But Brother Malcolm was noticeably absent. When he was present, he was regulated to a minute caption or a passing reference.

What a great tragedy.

What happens to the legacy of a public figure after their demise says more about those left to be caretakers of that legacy than the figures themselves? Malcolm X is an essential part of our story. Malcolm X's legacy must be rightly protected and preserved for the benefit of future generations. And unfortunately, we must admit that as a collective community, we have not done a good job where Brother Malcolm is concerned.

We have not done right by Brother Malcolm, who did so much right for us. If we don't protect and safeguard this legacy, how will present and future generations know, as Brother

Malcolm taught us, that "the future belongs to those who prepare for it today"? How will they know that "nobody can give you freedom"? How will they know that "nobody can give you equality or justice or anything. If you're a man, you take it," or that "I'm for truth, no matter who tells it. I'm for justice, no matter who it's for or against," or that "truth is on the side of the oppressed"?

How will we counter the self-hate that permeates so many of our communities? Did not Brother Malcolm inquire, "Who taught you to hate the color of your skin? Who taught you to hate the texture of your hair? Who taught you to hate the shape of your nose and the shape of your lips? Who taught you to hate yourself from the top of your head to the soles of your feet?"[35]

So, here is the pressing question: How much is Malcolm X's legacy worth? $10,000? $50,000? $100,000? $150,000? How committed are we to preserving his legacy for future generations? I told my brother Imam Omar that I know the request is for $200,000 tonight. Nevertheless, here in New York City, the birthplace of hip-hop, in the borough of Sean "Puffy" Combs, which stands upon Malcolm's revolutionary shoulders, with all the fame and resources of those who have been produced by this place, and with all who are watching this program across the world, anything less than $1 million would be a sin before God.

Tonight, we say we love Brother Malcolm. By the end of the night, we will see how much. God bless!

Wakanda Forever!
Hebrews 11:1–3

(Delivered February 6, 2019, in Dallas, Texas, for
the Black Seminarians Association of SMU Perkins School
of Theology's inaugural worship celebration in
commemoration of Black History Month.)

Without question, the most destructive force in the history of the world is the heresy of white supremacy. Because of white supremacy, entire nations of Indigenous people have been forever annihilated from the earth, aftereffects of the sin of stolen lands theologized as Manifest Destiny. Whole nations have been colonized and the people indigenous to those nations subjugated to economic, physical, political, social, and spiritual oppression.

It is the heresy of white supremacy that resulted in sun-kissed humanity being forced into chains, then crammed into the hulls of ships, where they were made to lie in one another's waste for the arduous odyssey across the sea. The sick and dying among them were callously cast overboard because their traffickers held insurance policies that allowed them to collect for slaves who died in transit but not for ill slaves who arrived safely to new lands.

White supremacy dragged Jewish people off to concentration camps and baked their bodies in ovens. White supremacy has sent bombs and heat-seeking missiles to rain down upon Brown, Asian, and yes, even Black youth in Philadelphia, the City of Brotherly Love.

White supremacy has sold bodies on the auction block, raped bodies in slave quarters, lynched bodies in trees, thrown bodies into rivers, burned down communities and business districts, criminalized bodies in the legislature, redlined bodies in segregated neighborhoods and projects, laid pipelines upon sacred land where bodies are buried, used bodies for unethical medical experiments, poisoned bodies with water supplies full of lead, defunded bodies in public schools, and erected idol gods called Confederate monuments in honor of white bodies, then blamed Black and Brown people's oppressed state upon an alleged inherent pathology known exclusively to themselves.

As such, there may be no nobler effort than the holy and sacred work of tearing down symbols and systems of white supremacy and of reimagining a world where white supremacy no longer exists. I believe that it is for this very reason that moviegoers across the globe flooded theaters for the cinematic release of Disney and Marvel Studios' *Black Panther*, one of the most significant pop culture phenomenons of 2018. It was also the highest-grossing film of 2018, earning over $700 million at the American box office and $1.3 billion globally. It currently ranks as the third-highest-grossing film of all time in the United States and the ninth-highest-grossing film in cinematic history. Even when adjusted for inflation, *Black Panther* will still rank among the ten highest-grossing films of the last thirty-five years. And just last month, it became the first superhero film to be nominated for an Oscar in the Best Picture category.

Even more important than its enormous economic gains was the fact that *Black Panther* imagined Wakanda, an African nation untouched by white supremacy, and dared to portray that land and its Black people as the wealthiest and most technologically advanced in the world. Moviegoers flooded theaters to lay eyes upon a world that does not yet exist, the greater fiction being not a land where vibranium exists but rather a land where Black people are fully free.

It is not lost on me that the Blackest fictional land was first created in the white mind of the recently departed Stan Lee. And this is not a stretch for me, for I believe that the very reason white people colonized many African countries was the wealth and beauty they possessed. The continent of Africa, the birthplace of human life, was also once the most technologically advanced in the world—the very grounds from which medicine, astronomy, mathematics, and the great sciences sprang forth. So, it is not a stretch to envision the wealthiest and most advanced land in the world remaining so, had it not been invaded and decimated by white supremacy.

Still, Stan Lee was not the first to envision such a land. Imagining the possibilities of a world void of white supremacy has long been the legacy and gift of Black people to the world. That great nineteenth-century womanist theologian and abolitionist Sojourner Truth, who lived during the days of American slavery, envisioned a world untouched by white supremacy when she boldly proclaimed, "I can now live the dream. I am the seed of the free, and I know it. I intend to bear great fruit." She also liberated her Christian faith from the bonds of white supremacy and patriarchy when she boldly declared, "Where did your Christ come from? From God and a woman! Man had nothing to do with him."[36]

The great twentieth-century human rights advocate and organizer Ella Baker, who lived during the days of Jim Crow, envisioned the work associated with creating a world untouched by white supremacy when she dared to affirm, "Remember, we are not fighting for the freedom of the Negro alone, but for the freedom of the human spirit, a larger freedom that encompasses all mankind."[37]

Certainly, the Reverend Martin Luther King Jr. envisioned a world untouched by white supremacy when he prophetically uttered, "I have a dream that my four little children will one day live in a nation where they will not be judged by the color of their skin but by the content of their character."

And there is still great need today for people to hold tight to the vision of a world void of white supremacy, especially in a country where white supremacist groups have increased their membership rolls by 30 percent in just the first two years of this white supremacist presidential administration. There is still a need for people to hold tight to the vision of a world void of white supremacy in a country where Dr. King's words and images have been largely co-opted by forces opposed to his radical vision of justice.

There is still a need for people to hold tight to the vision of a world void of white supremacy in a country where

- fifty years after Dr. King's death, the legacy of redlining and unfair housing remains, and there are fewer Black homeowners today than in 1968
- incarceration rates have increased by 700 percent with the War on Drugs, wherein laws were purposely designed to ensnare Black, Brown, and poor bodies
- the laws are only now changing because of an opioid crisis among whites
- thousands of Black and Brown people remain incarcerated for selling drugs, many now legal, drugs that are earning primarily white people outrageous profits in many states
- our public schools have been virtually resegregated since 1988
- Black unemployment remains nearly twice as high as it is for other racial groups
- economists report that there is such a massive racial wealth disparity in America that it would take 228 years for median Black family wealth to equate to that of median white family wealth
- statistically, there has been little to no actual economic progress for Black people in America since Martin Luther King began the Poor People's Campaign over a half century ago

Yes, there is still a need for people to hold tight to the vision of a world void of white supremacy, especially in a city such as Dallas, where

- Black people comprise only 25 percent of the population but 50 percent of all arrests and nearly 70 percent of the homeless population.

- Black people earn just 54 cents to the dollar of white people.
- Fifteen percent of the city's tax base is in the Black and Brown southern sector and 85 percent is in the majority-white northern sector.
- Fifty percent of the population cannot afford their basic needs in the city the Urban Institute named the most racially segregated and racially inequitable city in America!

How is it possible to hew a global Wakanda—a place of freedom, prosperity, and health for all people—out of a global hell where white supremacist foreign policies have displaced more people from their homelands than at any point in the history of the world? Well, it requires what is has always required: faith in God and in the work of God through God's people.

Hebrews 11 is widely considered to be greatest treatise on faith in the Bible. It was written around A.D. 67 to its original audience of Hebrew Christians who were facing persecution so great that many of them were considering giving up their new faith and returning to Judaism. The writer needed to present Christ as perfect and superior to their opponents to give these Christians the courage to fight on and not turn away from their salvation.

And since our salvation is secured by our faith, the Hebrews writer wastes no time speaking on the matter of faith in this chapter: "Faith is the substance of things hoped for, it is the evidence of things we cannot see. Through their faith, the people in days of old earned a good reputation. By faith we understand that the entire universe was formed at God's command, that what we now see did not come from anything that can be seen."

Then the writer offers a presentation of many of the heroes of scripture and the faith they displayed. "It was by faith that Abel brought a more acceptable offering to God than Cain did. Abel's offering gave evidence that he was a righteous man, and God showed his approval of his gifts. Although Abel is long dead, he still speaks to us by his example of faith. It was by faith that

Enoch was taken up to heaven without dying ..." He disappeared because God took him. "For before he was taken up, he was known as a person who pleased God."

Then, before continuing with his presentation of faith, the writer makes a bold proclamation of the necessity of faith. He writes,

And it is impossible to please God without faith. Anyone who wants to come to him must believe that God exists and that he rewards those who sincerely seek him. It was by faith that Noah built a large boat to save his family from the flood. He obeyed God, who warned him about things that had never happened before. By his faith Noah condemned the rest of the world, and he received the righteousness that comes by faith.

It was by faith that Abraham obeyed when God called him to leave home and go to another land that God would give him as his inheritance. He went without knowing where he was going. And even when he reached the land God promised him, he lived there by faith—for he was like a foreigner, living in tents. And so, did Isaac and Jacob, who inherited the same promise. Abraham was confidently looking forward to a city with eternal foundations, a city designed and built by God.

It was by faith that even Sarah was able to have a child, though she was barren and was too old. She believed that God would keep his promise. And so a whole nation came from this one man who was as good as dead—a nation with so many people that, like the stars in the sky and the sand on the seashore, there is no way to count them.

All these people died still believing what God had promised them. They did not receive what was promised, but they saw it all from a distance and welcomed it. They agreed that they were foreigners and nomads here on earth. Obviously people who say such things are looking forward to a country they can call their own. If they had longed for the country they came from, they could have gone back. But they were looking for a better place, a heavenly homeland. That is why God is not ashamed to be called their God, for he has prepared a city for them.

It was by faith that Abraham offered Isaac as a sacrifice when God was testing him. Abraham, who had received God's promises, was ready to sacrifice his only son, Isaac, even though God had told him, "Isaac is the son through whom your descendants will be counted." Abraham reasoned that if Isaac died, God was able to bring him back to life again. And in a sense, Abraham did receive his son back from the dead. It was by faith that Isaac promised blessings for the future to his sons, Jacob and Esau.

It was by faith that Jacob, when he was old and dying, blessed each of Joseph's sons and bowed in worship as he leaned on his staff. It was by faith that Joseph, when he was about to die, said confidently that the people of Israel would leave Egypt. He even commanded them to take his bones with them when they left. It was by faith that Moses' parents hid him for three months when he was born. They saw that God had given them an unusual child, and they were not afraid to disobey the king's command.

It was by faith that Moses, when he grew up, refused to be called the son of Pharaoh's daughter. He chose to share the oppression of God's people instead of enjoying the fleeting pleasures of sin. 26He thought it was better to suffer for the sake of Christ than to own the treasures of Egypt, for he was looking ahead to his great reward. It was by faith that Moses left the land of Egypt, not fearing the king's anger. He kept right on going because he kept his eyes on the one who is invisible. It was by faith that Moses commanded the people of Israel to keep the Passover and to sprinkle blood on the doorposts so that the angel of death would not kill their firstborn sons.

It was by faith that the people of Israel went right through the Red Sea as though they were on dry ground. But when the Egyptians tried to follow, they were all drowned.

It was by faith that the people of Israel marched around Jericho for seven days, and the walls came crashing down. It was by faith that Rahab the prostitute was not destroyed with the people in her city who refused to obey God. For she had given a friendly welcome to the spies.

How much more do I need to say? It would take too long to recount the stories of the faith of Gideon, Barak, Samson, Jephthah, David, Samuel, and all the prophets. By faith these people overthrew kingdoms, ruled with justice, and received what God had promised them. They shut the mouths of lions, quenched the flames of fire, and escaped death by the edge of the sword. Their weakness was turned to strength. They became strong in battle and put whole armies to flight.

Women received their loved ones back again from death. But others were tortured, refusing to turn from God in order to be set free. They placed their hope in a better life after the resurrection. Some were jeered at, and their backs were cut open with whips. Others were chained in prisons. Some died by stoning, some were sawed in half, and others were killed with the sword. Some went about wearing skins of sheep and goats, destitute and oppressed and mistreated. They were too good for this world, wandering over deserts and mountains, hiding in caves and holes in the ground.

All these people earned a good reputation because of their faith, yet none of them received all that God had promised. For God had something better in mind for us, so that they would not reach perfection without us.

Our people made it through slavery by faith, Jim Crow by faith, lynching by faith, bombings by faith, assassination of our leaders by faith, redlining by faith, the Flint water crisis by faith, LA uprisings by faith, the KKK by faith, corrupt cops by faith, the prison industrial complex by faith, the school-to-prison pipeline by faith, stop and frisk by faith, the alt-right by faith.

This does not even include the other struggles and strivings faced by the whole of humanity upon this terrestrial plain: the heights of ecstasy, the depths of despair, joy-filled mornings, sleepless nights, the expected and the unanticipated—the vicissitudes of life. Yet, we still stand.

Might I suggest that, in accordance to the witness and testimony of scripture, our Wakanda and our vibranium, the substance that has held us together and that keeps us strong in the face of many obstacles, is none other than our faith in God? Is there anybody who is willing to say, "I am living by faith, walking by faith, standing by faith, believing by faith, praying by faith, and trusting by faith? As matter of fact, we've come this far by faith, leaning on the LORD, trusting in his holy word, and he has not failed me yet. Can't turn around. We have come this far by faith!"

Somebody here may even want to get personal: "I made it through addiction by faith, my divorce by faith, that assault by faith, that sickness by faith, through my layoff by faith. Almost lost my mind, but I kept it by faith; almost lost my joy, but I kept it by faith; almost lost my peace, but I kept it by faith!"

What I love about *Black Panther* is that when they need to release more power, they cross themselves. In Greek, the X-like letter Χ is called *chi*. The Χ was the symbol used for Christ. I dare you to cross yourself, tap into your faith, and when we break open our cross, release your power into the world Say yes!

I'm All the Way Up!
Genesis 1:26–31

(Delivered January 11, 2017, in Los Angeles, California, as revivalist for the Theology in the Hood Conference.)

Scientific racism is defined as "the use of ostensibly scientific or pseudoscientific techniques and hypotheses to support or justify the belief in racism, racial inferiority, racialism, or racial superiority."[38]

Scientific racism seeks to classify human populations into "physically discrete human races that might be asserted to be superior or inferior." Such dubious efforts date back to the fifth century BC and the work of Hippocrates, known as the "Father of Western Medicine," and to whom is credited the Hippocratic Oath. In his work *Airs, Waters, and Places*, Hippocrates states that "dark people are cowards, and light people courageous fighters."

During the French Enlightenment, Voltaire, a French writer, historian, and philosopher, stated, "Our wise men have said that man was created in the image of God. Now here is a lovely image of the Divine Maker: a flat and wide nose with little or hardly any intelligence." In jest, Voltaire argued that being Black was incompatible with being made in the image of God. He claimed that our natural features were far too repulsive and that we lacked the necessary intellectual capacity to reflect God.

Scientific racism—along with its theological underpinnings, as supported by Eurocentric conceptions of the Divine—has been one of the most destructive forces in the history of the world. Eurocentric conceptions of the Divine supporting white supremacist notions can be credited with causing innumerable atrocities. It was used to justify the horrors of European colonialism, which destroyed ancient kingdoms upon the Mother Continent. It was used to justify the horrors of American slavery, which separated families, raped men, women, and children, and while in transit threw millions of souls overboard to dwell within watery graves. Yes, even South African apartheid was supported by such alarming conceptions of the Divine.

Although scientific racism is deemed pseudoscientific, its influence continues, as masses of people still believe that they are superior to others based upon their race. The currents that continue to flow from this poisonous stream is what emboldened an overzealous, armed neighborhood watch volunteer to kill a teenager armed with Skittles and iced tea. It is what encouraged a white twenty-one-year-old stranger to walk into a Black church concealing a .45-caliber semiautomatic handgun, sit with the pastor and parishioners in Bible study, and then unleash a horrid hail of bullets, killing nine faithful and kind Christians. It is what causes school districts and the military to ban our natural hairstyles as unprofessional. It is even what causes some people to be upset when a Black first lady speaks about her Black daughters playing outside on the White House lawn—a house built by Black people.

Dare I say that the Eurocentric notion of God as white is fundamentally responsible for the rejection of President Barack Hussein Obama during his terms in office and the ready embrace of President Donald J. Trump by over 80 percent of white evangelicals? Donald Trump is a white man

- with no previous military or political experience,
- who is routinely sued for unethical business practices,
- who has been accused of the sexual assault of a minor,
- who was recorded on tape bragging about sexually assaulting women,
- who knows nothing about the faith his supporters claim to hold so dear,
- who, according to *The Atlantic*, represents a bigoted, misogynistic worldview and an "existential threat" to the security of our nation,
- whose frequent, verified lies to the American public have ushered in an era termed post-truth,
- whose campaign is now accused of collaborating with a hostile foreign government to influence an American election.

Yes, the notion of whiteness as rightness has been destructive on many planes, but possibly never more so than when it is internalized in the Black soul. It has accomplished no less than to help breed self-hate, and self-hate remains one of the greatest barriers to building and sustaining movements today.

Self-hate breeds distrust of any and everybody who looks like you. Self-hate will cause you to sabotage yourself or to sabotage your brother or sister if you feel as though they are getting ahead of you. Self-hate will cause you to make enemies of friends and friends of enemies. Whiteness as rightness has been a frontal attack on Black bodies, Black minds, and Black emotions; but most of all, it has been an attack on Black souls. Who can forget the prophetic inclinations of W. E. B. Du Bois, who wrote, "It is a peculiar sensation, this double-consciousness, this sense of always looking at one's self through the eyes of others, of measuring one's soul by the tape of a world that looks on in amused contempt and pity."[39]

It seeks to question our epistemology, our origins, and our self-worth. All of this has been used as anesthesia to put us to sleep, to cause us to feel inadequate, undesirable, and unfit. There is no greater way to defeat a people than to cause them to believe that they are nothing and that they came from nothing.

The same is true spiritually. There is no more effective way to defeat a person spiritually than to make them think that they are nothing or that they came from nothing. Every day, I encounter people who don't know who they are, whose they are, and what they have been purposed to do. Although we may have recently spent much time talking about the current presidential administration and his threats to public life, we have not spent enough time talking about the self-hatred that breeds divisions and fractures in our community, which will keep us from mounting an effective countermovement.

I believe that as we consider this text, we discover that we inherently possess great value and worth—despite the enemy's attempt to make us feel otherwise, for while we were once asleep, we are now all the way up!

The book of Genesis is the ultimate epistemological book. It tells us about the origins of our world. The Bible says in Genesis 1 that the earth "was formless and empty, and darkness covered the deep waters" and that "the Spirit of God hovered over the surface of the waters. Then God spoke, 'Let there be light,' and there was light ... God spoke, 'Let there be a space between the waters, to separate the waters of the heavens from the waters of the earth,' and that is what happened" ... God spoke, 'Let the waters beneath the sky flow together into one place, so dry land may appear.' And that is what happened."

Every time God spoke, whatever God spoke came to pass— seed-bearing plants, waters filled with fish, animals upon the land.

However, in verse 26, God's use of language changes drastically. Instead of saying "let there be," God says, "Let us make": "Then God said, 'Let us make human beings in our image, to be like us. They will reign over the fish in the sea, the birds in the sky, the livestock, all the wild animals on the earth, and the small animals that scurry along the ground.' So, God created human beings in his own image. In the image of God, he created them; male and female he created them. Then God blessed them and said, 'Be fruitful and multiply. Fill the earth and govern it. Reign over the fish in the sea, the birds in the sky, and all the animals that scurry along the ground.' Then God said, 'Look! I have given you every seed-bearing plant throughout the earth and all the fruit trees for your food. And I have given every green plant as food for all the wild animals, the birds in the sky, and the small animals that scurry along the ground—everything that has life.' And that is what happened."

As we consider this text, there are some gifts that God immediately gives to those whom God has created in God's own image. First, God gifts them with affirmation. God looked over what God had made and affirmed that it was good.

God gifts them with accommodation. Before God created them, God created everything they needed to thrive. God says, "Look! I have given you every seed-bearing plant throughout the earth and all the fruit trees for your food."

God gifts them with accreditation. Accreditation means that "to give official authorization or approval of." God said, "Be fruitful and multiply. Fill the earth and govern it. Reign over the fish in the sea, the birds in the sky, and all the animals that scurry along the ground."

However, even with the affirmation, accommodation, and accreditation, a controversy still emerges in the text. In the second chapter account of the creation, we find that God looks upon the first human and declares it was not good for him to be alone. The Bible says that "the LORD caused the man to fall into a deep sleep." I know what you are thinking. If God had fully affirmed him, fully accommodated him, and fully accredited him, why would God seem to suggest that he was deficient in some way? Why would God put him to sleep?

But I have good news. When the systems of this world—racism, classism, xenophobia—put you to sleep, they attempt to leave you in a state of self-hate; but anytime God puts you to sleep, it is to prepare you for greater glory! For the Bible says that while the man slept, "the LORD God took one of his ribs and closed the opening. Then the LORD God made a woman from the rib and he brought her to the man."

The man was not defiant. The man lacked nothing. God simply put him to sleep to pull out from him what was already living inside him. And when the man connected to the power brought out from him, a power he already possessed, together they produced more vessels with more power!

I dare you to declare to any heartache that you have ever felt, any enemy that has ever stood in your way, any challenge that comes before you, "I'm all the way up! I am asleep no more!"

I am so grateful that awake people produce awake people. If you know you are awake, if you claim God's affirmation, accommodation, and accreditation for your life, then let's get in formation.

When you see yourself as God has made you, you can proclaim to the world, "I woke up like this!"

I am fearfully and wonderfully made! I woke up like this!

I am the head and not the tail! I woke up like this!

God has supplied all my needs according to his riches in glory! I woke up like this!

No weapon formed against me shall prosper! I woke up like this!

All things are working together for my good! I woke up like this!

Surely goodness and mercy shall follow me all the days of my life! I woke up like this!

Now all the awake people give God praise and declare:

I am awake to new power!

I am awake to new possibilities!

I am awake to fresh anointing!

I am awake to new mercy!

I am awake to unspeakable joy!

I am awake to unstoppable peace!

I am awake to my next level in God!

I'm all the way up!

If These Walls Could Talk
Daniel 5:22–28

(Delivered September 27, 2020, in Dallas, Texas,
following the failure to indict the police officers who murdered
Breonna Taylor in Louisville, Kentucky, on March 13, 2020.)

On May 29, 1851, Sojourner Truth, the iconic nineteenth-century womanist and abolitionist, uttered these words in a speech:

> That man over there says that women need to be helped into carriages, and lifted over ditches, and to have the best place everywhere. Nobody ever helps me into carriages, or over mud-puddles, or gives me any best place! And ain't I a woman? Look at me! Look at my arm! I have ploughed and planted, and gathered into barns, and no man could head me! And ain't I a woman? I could work as much and eat as much as a man—when I could get it—and bear the lash as well! And ain't I a woman? I have borne five children, and seen most all sold off to slavery, and when I cried out with my mother's grief, none but Jesus heard me! And ain't I a woman.

In her 1937 epic novel *Their Eyes Were Watching God*, Zora Neale Hurston penned these disturbing words spoken through Janie, the book's protagonist: "De nigger woman is de mule uh de world so fur as Ah can see."

In 1962, Malcolm X offered this troubling assessment: "The most disrespected person in America is the Black woman. The most unprotected person in America is the Black woman. The most neglected person in America is the Black woman."

And this week in Louisville, Kentucky, we bore witness to yet another travesty of justice regarding the lives of Black women as a police officer was indicted for wanton endangerment. This happens when a person "wantonly engages in conduct which creates substantial danger of death or serious physical injury to another person."

Since March 13, there have been demands for justice in America and across the world in response to the murder of Breonna Taylor, yet the lone officer indicted was not charged for the murder of Breonna Taylor. Instead, he was charged for firing shots into her walls, endangering the lives of her neighbors. No one would be held accountable for murdering a sleeping Black woman. The only crime committed was engaging in behavior that had the potential to harm those around the dead young woman. Even in the final written report there was mention of walls before there was any mention of this Black woman whose life was taken far too soon. When the report finally did reference her, it did not do so by name. Say her name.

Since Breonna Taylor's voice was silenced, literally and physically, I thought it would be interesting if we might interrogate the walls.

The Bible says that one day King Belshazzar, leader of the Babylonian Empire, held a feast for one thousand nobles where he ordered wine be served to his guests out of the gold cups that had been taken from the temple of Jerusalem when the Babylonians conquered the city.

This was an affront to God, using that which had been consecrated as holy to engage in revelry. To make matters worse, as they drank from the cups, they began to worship their idol gods—gods made of gold, silver, bronze, iron, wood, and stone.

It was then that the king lifted his eyes and saw an usual sight: the appearance of fingers on a disembodied hand writing on the wall of the palace near the lampstand so that he might see the words clearly.

The king was terrified. He turned pale, and lost strength in his legs. He called for his astrologers and fortune-tellers to interpret the writing, but they were unable to do so. That is when the queen mother heard what was transpiring and came to King Belshazzar. She told him about a man his father Nebuchadnezzar knew well, a man of God named Daniel who had "insight, understanding, and wisdom like the gods." Daniel was a man his father had placed above all the musicians, enchanters, and fortune-tellers in his day. He was a man who could "interpret dreams, explain riddles, and solve difficult problems."

I think there is something to be said about a national leader who is completely out of touch with the nation's history, a leader so inept that he did not bother to consult the seasoned wisdom already present in the kingdom. A leader who surrounded himself with other leaders who were unable to lead the nation in the direction it should go.

When Daniel was brought before Belshazzar, the king declared that if Daniel could interpret the wall, he would be clothed in purple, adorned with gold, and made the third highest ruler in the kingdom.

Daniel essentially responded, "Keep your stuff, but I will let you know what these walls are saying."

> You are his successor, O Belshazzar, and you knew all this, yet you have not humbled yourself. For you have proudly defied the Lord of heaven and have had these cups from his Temple brought before you. You and your nobles and your wives and concubines have been drinking wine from them while praising gods of silver, gold, bronze, iron, wood, and stone—gods that neither see nor hear nor know anything at all. But you have not honored the God who gives you the breath of life and controls your destiny! So, God has sent this hand to write this message.

> This is the message that was written: "MENE, MENE, TEKEL, and PARSIN." This is what these words mean: *Mene* means "numbered." God has numbered the days of your reign and has brought it to an end. *Tekel* means "weighed." You have been weighed

on the balances and have not measured up. *Parsin* means "divided." Your kingdom has been divided and given to the Medes and Persians.

Now here a controversy arises in the text. These words are Aramaic, words that would have been readily known to educated people like the other astrologers and fortune-tellers at that time. But they were unable to read them. One scholar suggests that these words were written in an ancient script then like the ancient Hebrew script. Thus, because Daniel was familiar with the script, he could read the walls.

I want to suggest that those rooted in the Word of God, in the script, can clearly read the walls. And if the walls of America could talk, I think they would utter the same thing that we find here in this text, if we continue along our current path.

Mene, Mene, America, your days are numbered and your position in the world is diminished. You can't continue to break Black, Brown, and Indigenous bodies in the streets and call yourself blessed. You can't continue to place profits above people's lives and call yourself blessed. You can't perform forced hysterectomies on refugees and call yourself blessed.

Tekel, America, you have been weighed on the balances, but you have not measured up. The greatness of a nation is not known by its military might but by how it treats its neighbors, by how it treats the stranger, by how it treat widows and orphans, and by how it treats the poor. America, you are not measuring up.

Parsin, America, we are already divided. Red states, blue states; Black people, white people; rich, poor; and somewhere I read that a house divided against itself cannot stand.

The walls are talking, but are we listening? The walls compel us to get our houses in order, but are we paying attention? The walls implore us to change now, but do we care?

The walls are talking.

We had better take heed.

PROPHETIC PROCLAMATIONS

Can I Live?

(Delivered June 19, 2019, in Wichita, Kansas, at the annual citywide Juneteenth celebration at Wichita State University.)

For the past month, the nation has been captivated by the American drama miniseries *When They See Us*, produced by acclaimed Black film director Ava DuVernay. It was the most-watched series on Netflix for thirteen straight days following its release. This gripping series is based on the true story of five Black teenagers residing in New York City in 1989. These young men were falsely accused of a heinous crime and sentenced to many years in prison before they ultimately were exonerated. During their interrogation and trial, their constitutional and civil rights were violated repeatedly. They suffered physical abuse, mental abuse, and even starvation in the process.

Recently, the National Registry of Exonerations released its report noting the false convictions that have been overturned in America since 1989. The numbers are startling, for it is only a representation of known false convictions overturned, not of all false convictions. The unspoken terror is that many more falsely accused remain behind bars and may never see the light of day. Although Black people make up just 12 percent of this nation's population, we are overrepresented in this group, which is true of every death-dealing reality in this nation. Of the 2,265 exonerees, 46 percent are Black; 56 percent of the 20,080 years of life lost behind bars, over twenty millennia, belongs to Black people.

On April 20, 2015, *The New York Times* released an equally disturbing report. One and a half million Black men between the ages of 25 and 54—the years considered to be prime in a man's working life—are missing from public life, dead, or in prison. That amounts to more than the number of American casualties in every war in which this nation has participated. A city of 1.5 million residents would be America's seventh-largest city, with only seventy thousand fewer residents than Phoenix or Philadelphia.

Four hundred years ago this August, the first twenty kidnapped Africans arrived in chains upon these shores, thus marking the entry of the transatlantic slave trade upon the land we now call America. Of the estimated 12 million Africans sold into slavery, an estimated 1.5 million Africans lost their lives in transit between the sixteenth and nineteenth centuries, some tossed overboard while still alive because slave traffickers could collect money through slave insurance for all Africans lost in transit, but not for those who arrived sick and unable to work.

This Monday marked the fourth anniversary of the massacre at Mother Emanuel AME Church. Nine people—three Black men and six Black women, including an eighty-seven-year-old—were shot and killed in cold blood during Bible study. My dear friend Rev. Risher lost her seventy-one-year-old mother that night. Ethel Lance was shot eight times at point-blank range.

While we will never know the magnitude of Black people who disappeared into the criminal justice system due to false accusations or unjust sentencing, or the magnitude of Black people thrown overboard into watery graves, or the magnitude of Black people murdered at the hands of white supremacists, it appears that Black death in America has been continuous—so much so that it is unquantifiable.

Therefore, when we consider the narrative experience of Black Americans and the African Diaspora, it has been an existential struggle. Our perpetual fight has been to live amid a myriad of systems and terrors designed to rob us of our lives. As the great James Weldon Johnson penned over a century ago, "We have come over a way that with tears has been watered. We have come, treading our path through the blood of the slaughtered."

When we consider the Black American experience today, we have come along an arduous path. For it was not 1918, not 1950, not 1963, but 2018 that recorded the single greatest year of hate crimes and racial violence.

We are now fifty years removed from the Kerner Commission report—created by the executive order of President Lyndon Baines Johnson—which said that white society is "deeply implicated in the ghetto. White institutions created it, white institutions maintain it, and white society condones it."

And fifty years since, there are fewer Black homeowners today than there were in 1968. Public schools have virtually resegregated since 1988. Unemployment and underemployment rates remain virtually unchanged. There are more Black men incarcerated than in college. Redlining continues across the country. Billions of dollars have been robbed from Black Americans because of the underappraisal of their homes. Infant mortality and the Black maternal death rate are on the rise.

Race inequity is so rabid in this nation that though Black American women are the most educated demographic in the United States, they are among the lowest paid in this country. Wealth disparity is so great in this nation that it would take 228 years for the median wealth of a Black family to equate to that of a white family, but only if white wealth ceases to increase.

Can we live?

Dr. King inquired, "What good is having the right to sit at a lunch counter if you can't afford to buy a burger?"

Can we live?

Dr. King said, "Freedom is never voluntarily given by the oppressor; it must be demanded by the oppressed."[40] Friends, it often appears that we have an illusion of freedom while still abiding in chains.

Black people are still dying of the effects of poisoned water in Flint. Unarmed Black people are still dying at the hands of police.

Can we live?

If we gather for a picnic, the police are called on us. If we are mowing grass, the police are called on us. If we have a business meeting in Starbucks, the police are called on us. If we fall asleep in the common area of our own dorm, the police are called on us. Entering our own homes or standing in our own backyards, the police are called on us.

Can we live?

Juneteenth is an important yet intriguing holiday. We rightfully celebrate the emancipation of Black people in Texas from the bonds of slavery. But there are two historical facts that cannot be overlooked related to the same. One is that the promise of freedom was intentionally delayed for economic gain, to bring in the final harvest. Some enslaved were not set free because their bondage provides others with economic gain.

Secondly, in Texas alone, according to Joyce King, author of *Hate Crime: The Story of a Dragging in Jasper, Texas*, who has documented lynching in Texas up to the 1998 lynching of James Byrd, four hundred former slaves were lynched in Texas alone in the years immediately following the first Juneteenth.

It appears that even after your freedom has been declared there are terrors and systems dedicated to ending your life.

That is why we must come to this moment with clear eyes. Instead of freedom attained, I submit that Juneteenth ought to be a celebration of freedom in progress. Praise God we are not where we used to be, but surely, we are not yet where we ought to be. Today, we celebrate and acknowledge those who came before us, whose courage and sacrifices have secured for us the world we have today. We call their names: Sojourner Truth, Ida B. Wells, Fannie Lou Hamer, Malcolm X, James Cone, and many others. We also acknowledge the ancestors whose names we will never know, names long forgotten in history, who made invaluable contributions all the same.

But we must acknowledge that we are not yet fully free to live. Tamir Rice taught us that. Sandra Bland taught us that. Botham Jean taught us that.

How can we live amid a myriad of systems and terrors explicitly designed to rob us of our lives?

We must keep fighting! We must keep resisting! We must keep building! We can't give up. We must openly declare in each season and in every generation that we shall live and that we shall be free. We must speak those things that are not as though they were, and we must continue working until it comes into being.

Reconcile or Resist?

(Delivered October 6, 2017, in Detroit, Michigan, for the Christian Community Development Association's national conference.)

I have been invited to speak to you tonight about racial reconciliation. However, if I were to speak to you tonight about racial reconciliation, I would do you a disservice. As a matter of fact, if racial reconciliation is your greatest aspiration for our nation, you likely are taking an odyssey down the wrong path.

The notion of racial reconciliation begs the question: To whom or with what are we being reconciled? If it is some notion of people of different hues skipping together through the meadows—which is most often the case—then it is a notion that not only lacks compassion and empathy, but also one that proves detrimental to the very future of our society.

Racial reconciliation is not manifested by your annual pulpit swap. There is no amount of MLK Day services or Black history programs that can bring it into being. It is not accomplished because you adopted a school, have a homeless ministry, or even provide some affordable housing.

While these things are good, they are not a solution to America's race problem. Neither are they a means of reconciliation. To whom or to what are we being reconciled?

Are we to reconcile with a presidential administration that has difficulty differentiating between Nazis and white supremacists as manifestations of evil versus those who would stand up for the sacred worth of humanity?

Are we to reconcile with an economic system literally built upon the backs of human beings born into slavery and the diabolical legacies of redlining, wherein the median wealth of a white family is $142,000 and rising, but the median wealth of a Black family is $11,000 and falling, and it will take 228 years for them to be made equal?

Are we to reconcile with the endless stream of blood flowing down America's streets as unarmed Black, Brown, and Native bodies are felled by police?

What most people desire when they speak of racial reconciliation is falsified peace, an illusion of comfort. They want Rodney King's "can we all get along?" They want an Obama beer summit. They dare to say, "Let's have a colorblind society," though our God is not colorblind, yet God loves us all the same.

Instead, let's get healed tonight.

Dr. King said, "True peace is not merely the absence of tension; it's the presence of justice." And to obtain justice, not only do we need resilience, we also need resistance.

When this year began in Dallas, there was a Muslim ban. And we resisted. When our Latinx brothers and sisters were harmed by ICE and threats of deportation, we resisted. When Fred Bradford Jr.'s murderer, Officer Brad Burgess, was acquitted of all charges, we resisted. When young Jordan Edwards had a bullet placed in his head by Officer Roy Oliver, we resisted. When monuments erected to white supremacy sought to lengthen their stay, we resisted. We showed our resilience by continuing to show up as a life-giving community to resist evil, knowing that when you resist evil, it must flee.

White supremacy takes no days off, and neither can we in our struggle. We are a people whose resilience has been made known in resistance. We are the conductors along the Underground Railroad, the standard of resistance to slavery with resilience. We are those who dared to build churches, businesses, schools, and homes, even when we were taken from those homes and lynched, even when our business districts were burned to the ground, and even when our churches were burned and bombed.

Through Jim Crow, we resist. Through Emmett Till, we resist. Through four little girls in Birmingham, we resist. Through Medgar, Malcolm, and Martin, we resist.

Through the War on Us—not the War on Drugs—mass incarceration, mandatory minimums, and militarized police, we resist.

Our resistance not only proves our resilience but is also a marker of the grace of God. It proves that if God be for you, who can be against you? It proves that no weapon formed shall prosper. We still worship at Sixteenth Street Baptist Church in Birmingham and at Mother Emanuel AME Church in Charleston.

We dare to declare that the Spirit of the Lord is upon us because God has anointed us to preach good news to the captive and recovery of sight to the blind, to let the oppressed go free, to declare the year of the Lord's favor! Let us continue to resist every form of white supremacy until justice flows like waters, and righteousness like a mighty stream!

Hands Up!
Psalm 28:1–2

(Delivered February 20, 2017, in Dallas, Texas, at the CrossTalk Conference at the SMU Perkins School of Theology.)

The summer of 2014 will be forever etched in the annals of history as one of the most violent and racially polarizing in American history.

Fifty years removed from Freedom Summer, when three young civil rights workers were brutally murdered outside Philadelphia, Mississippi, over the course of a month and a half this year at least five unarmed African American males were killed by police officers in this country.

On July 17, Eric Garner, forty-three, was strangled to death by officers in Staten Island, New York, for the crime of allegedly selling untaxed cigarettes.

On August 5, twenty-two-year-old John Crawford was shot to death in a Beavercreek, Ohio, Walmart by officers while holding a BB gun he had picked off the store's shelf to purchase.

And on August 11, Ezell Ford was fatally shot in the back by officers while lying on the ground in South-Central Los Angeles.

Although the lives of these young Black men were callously discounted, all life is precious, given as a trust from God, and the untimely loss of any life is tragic. Our nation and our international community were deeply troubled by the shooting and death of eighteen-year-old Michael Brown on August 9 in Ferguson, Missouri.

We were troubled, and not only by the fact that he was a teenager just a few days away from entering college. The way in which he died shook us to our core.

He was shot at over ten times and hit six times, with two entry wounds in his head, including one through the very apex of his head. Yet, not only was he unarmed, eyewitness accounts also attest that he was shot while his hands were raised.

Raised hands is the universal sign of surrender. Hands raised declare, "I am unarmed, and I am of no threat to you." Hands raised declare, "I voluntarily give myself over to your authority, and I am at your mercy."

Yet, even with hands raised, young Michael Brown was shot dead and left lying in the street for over four hours. In the wake of his death, protests emerged, mostly peaceful, but some violent, and all passionate, because of the troubling nature of Brown's death and the overall culture of police persecution in that area.

And just when we thought it could not get any worse—and so that we would know that we are not immune to such tragedies—only twenty miles east of here, in Forney, Texas, Kametra Barbour and her two children and two godchildren were pulled over by Forney police, who drew their guns and forced Ms. Barbour out of her car. They made her walk backward with her hands above her head. Police then lied to her, saying she had been positively identified as a driver with a gun, though the 911 call reported a different car color, make, and model, and four adult males, not one woman with four children under age ten.

Our hearts were broken again when her young son also emerged from the car, with hands raised, and inquired, "Are we being arrested?"

In response to all these tragic occurrences, we have felt like the late, great Marvin Gaye, who recorded his sentiments in his lyrics: "Crime is increasing / Trigger happy policing / Panic is spreading / God knows where, where we're heading / Oh, make me wanna holler / And throw up both my hands / Yeah, it makes me wanna holler / And throw up both my hands."[41]

Throw up my hands in disbelief. Throw up my hands in despair. Throw up my hands in frustration. Throw up my hands in exasperation. This can readily happen when we feel like there is no end in sight to our crisis, when we feel like we have tried all that we can to change our situations and predicaments, and our attempts have failed.

Psalm 28 is a psalm of distress. The psalmist has concern for the evil that surrounds him, and he seeks refuge in the sanctuary. Although he is in distress, there is still hope. How is it possible to be in distress and to be in hope at the same time?

The psalmist writes, "To you, Lord, I call. You are my Rock, do not turn a deaf ear to me. For if you remain silent, I will be like those who go down to the pit. Hear my cry for mercy as I call to you for help, as I lift up my hands toward your Most Holy Place."

Here we find one of the Hebrew words for hands up—*todaw*—which means "hands extended in praise."

First, the psalmist has hope because God is his rock. A rock is unshifting, unchanging, constant. Despite all that is going on, God is the same yesterday, today, and forever!

Second, he has hope because God hears our cry. If God can hear us, God can come and see about us.

Third, he has hope because he knows who has the power to help. He lifts his hands—in distress, but with hope. In surrender, but also in praise.

Times may be hard, but God is still good. That's good news! When I can't, God can!

The great eighteenth-century hymn writer Charles Wesley once penned in lyric, "Father, I stretch my hands to thee, no other help I know. If thou withdraw thyself from me, oh whither shall I go?"

The annals of history record another young man who was brutalized by a corrupt police state. He was conceived out of wedlock to a young mother. His people were subjugated and oppressed in a militarized police state.

The violence in his community was so great that his family had to flee to safety behind the borders of another country as refugees. When he was an adult, the system constantly tried to set him up to kill him. Simply for speaking the truth, a crowd tried to throw him off a cliff.

He ultimately was arrested on trumped-up charges and tried in a kangaroo court. He suffered police brutality and was beaten mercilessly. Without proper representation in the courts, he was sentenced to death. And when he arrived at the place of execution, they lynched him on a tree.

But the executioners did not understand who the condemned was; for if they did, they never would have had him put his hands up.

Those same hands had healed the sick!
Those same hands had raised the dead!
Those same hands had fed the hungry!
Those same hands had held back God's wrath and secured humanity's freedom from sin, death, and the grave!

So, when I feel like I cannot go on, I raise my hands to the one whose hands were raised for me at Calvary. And because God has been so good to me, I must raise my hands! *Todaw*, extended your hands!

For I lift my hands in total praise to you! "I love the Lord, he heard my cry / And pitied every groan, long as I live / And troubles rise, I hasten to his throne!"[42]

Hands up! Give God glory!
Hands up! Give God praise!
Hands up! Bless God's name!
Despite all perils, the LORD is great, and greatly to be praised!

Mourning Mothers, White Flowers, and Steep Steps to Justice

(An editorial published in *The Huffington Post* on May 14, 2017.)

When I arrived, they were already climbing the steep steps, a sea of red ascending in a somber procession. Leading the procession were the parents of Jordan Edwards, whose body had only been lowered in the ground a week prior. I hurriedly joined the procession, making it in time to help settle the wreath on the ground and to stand beside the family and the family's attorney.

The Edwards family was not alone. Present, too, were the families of other sons felled in fatal police encounters. On Mother's Day eve, as we stood together in front of the Frank Crowley Courts Building, one by one mourning mothers offered remembrances of their sons forever taken from their warm embrace.

The stairs ascending to the Crowley Building are indeed steep. Under a bright and sweltering sun, they appeared even steeper. The building itself resembles a fortress, unwelcoming and inhospitable to the very justice that we seek.

Yet, we remained undeterred. We were there not only to remember, but also to ensure that no more injustices come to the Edwards family or to any family still seeking justice for their loved one.

I stood beside one mother as she shared precious memories of her son. The weight of her grief swelled as she spoke until it became so heavy that she could no longer speak. Her legs appeared to weaken, and I began to worry that she might crumble to the ground under the tremendous weight that she carried. I held her up and walked her away—away from the crowd, away from the cameras—to the cool shade of nearby trees.

I embraced her. She rested her weary head in the cup of my shoulder. Then she wept. And wept. And wept bitterly. She wept until her weeping turned to moaning.

Then she moaned. And moaned. And moaned. And moaned. And moaned.

She moaned so deeply it felt as if she might uproot the trees surrounding us.

Then silence. She could moan no more.

I prayed with her and for her. When she regained her strength, we walked together to lay her white flowers upon the growing memorial. A sea of white flowers already adorned the pavement. Although such flowers are traditionally given on Mother's Day to those whose mothers have departed, this day, the mothers received white flowers in memory of their dearly departed sons.

Before I walked the mother over to the memorial, she did utter one phrase.

"Why, God?"

I did not offer a response; for I wondered the same.

It's Time to Resurrect the Radical King!

(An editorial published in the *Dallas Morning* News under the paper's chosen title "We Must Resurrect the True, Radical Legacy of Martin Luther King" on March 25, 2018.)

In the sixth chapter of the book of Hebrews—a New Testament letter dated a few decades after the crucifixion of Christ—the author, as he castigates a community of Christians for failing to adhere to the foundational principles of their new faith, presents a most horrific image of continuous brutalities suffered by Christ. Because of their failure to mature in the faith and repent of their evil deeds, the author found them guilty of no less than crucifying Christ again and again. The author levies upon them the additional accusation of repeatedly subjecting Christ to public shame.

What happens to the legacy of a public figure after death reveals more about the contemporary community serving as caretakers of that legacy than the public figure. Five decades ago, an assassin's bullet nearly severed the head of thirty-nine-year-old Dr. Martin Luther King Jr. as he stood on the balcony of the Lorraine Motel in Memphis, Tennessee. To now isolate King's assassination to a singular date in history is to miss the ways in which his legacy has continued to be crucified ever since.

Other than the Christ, no other name, image, or legacy has been so misused to advance an alternative vision than the one originally espoused than Dr. King's. Our American community of caretakers has all but robbed Dr. King of his prophetic words and ministry. We have sanitized his legacy, making him less radical in death than he was in life, using his words, meant to pierce the soul, to sell trucks during the Super Bowl.

This past January in Dallas, I was honored to host the Reverend William Barber—a man seen by many as walking most closely in the footsteps of Dr. King—over several days surrounding the King holiday. Barber continuously warned against further commemorations of Dr. King, especially by those who would be opposed to Dr. King's work and ministry if he were with us today.

In life, Dr. King was radically opposed to the tripartite evils of poverty, racism, and militarism. Yes, he had a dream that one day his children would live in a nation where they would not be judged by the hue of their skin but by the substance of their character. But King also dreamed of a guaranteed income for all Americans that would eradicate poverty.

Yes, Dr. King had a dream that "little Black boys and little Black girls [would be] able to join hands with little white boys and while girls as sisters and brothers." But Dr. King also declared, "We can never be satisfied as long as the Negro is the victim of the unspeakable horrors of police brutality." Dr. King did not just promote cosmetic change but also policy change, even voicing support for reparations through a "Bill of Rights for the Disadvantaged" to achieve racial equity in America.

Due to the totality of his radical dreams and hope for America, Dr. King was despised and largely unpopular, especially during the final years of his life. According to a 1968 Harris poll, at the time of his death Dr. King had a 75-percent disapproval rating among Americans.[43] Even in Dallas, Dr. King's presence and work was greatly opposed, as white business elites co-opted the Black religious establishment to quell and resist their community's pursuit of justice across the city. Today, those who would have been opposed to Dr. King's presence and work find opportunity to use his words out of context and recast his legacy as having the sole desire that "we all just get along."

In the name of justice, Dr. King brought city economies to their knees for failure to accommodate Black people equally. The buses of Montgomery did not desegregate, nor did the Birmingham downtown business district, because of the kindheartedness of white people. Desegregation came because Black economic boycotts nearly sent them into bankruptcy.

Dr. King did not merely ask for the right to vote; he demanded the right to vote. And he and thousands of others willingly submitted themselves to arrest through civil disobedience in pursuit of the same.

If Dr. King were alive today, he might pose some challenging questions to the city of Dallas. If Dallas is "diverse," "vibrant," and "progressive," as is penned on official City of Dallas memos, why does a sixty-foot-tall Confederate monument to white supremacy remain in view of Dallas City Hall on the grounds of the Dallas Convention Center, with the support of Dallas' "progressive" mayor?

Nearly 70 percent of Dallas' homeless population is Black. Why? That number is higher than the already daunting national average, for a demographic that only constitutes 13 percent of the American populace. How is it possible for Dallas to lead the nation in making new millionaires while leading the nation in concentrated communities of poverty and ranking near the top in the nation in childhood poverty?

Why have Black and Brown children been forced to attend schools with mold, poor water quality, and rodents? How is it that nearly fifty years after the Fair Housing Act redlining continues and Dallas remains residentially segregated? Why are many Black and Brown families abiding in substandard living conditions?

If we truly want to commemorate the life and legacy of Dr. King, we must resurrect Dr. King. Not as in the bodily resurrection of the crucified Christ, but a moral resurrection of the values and principles Dr. King exposed and was martyred in pursuit of.

We must pick up the mantle of Dr. King's Poor People's Campaign. We must enlist ourselves among the "drum majors of justice," the "creatively maladjusted," and the "disciplined nonconformists" who have always pushed forward the needle of justice in this nation and across the world.

We must recommit ourselves to speaking truth to power, even if that means power will seek to isolate, shun, and silence us in the process. And we must continue to do all these things and more, until justice flows like waters, and righteousness like a mighty stream."

If we do, Dr. King's true legacy will be resurrected to life again.

A Radical Dream

(Delivered August 28, 2017, in Dallas, Texas, before a prayer march to the Robert E. Lee monument in Lee Park.)

Today is a hallowed day in the collective memory of the African Diaspora in America, a day of great spectacle and celebration as well as a day of gut-wrenching pain. On this day in 1955, young Emmett Till's beaten, mutilated, and bullet-riddled body was found afloat in Mississippi's Tallahatchie River. On this day in 2008, Senator Barack Hussein Obama accepted the Democratic nomination in Denver, Colorado, en route to becoming the forty-fourth president of the United States of America. On this day in 1963, word reached America that W. E. B. Du Bois, the first Black American to earn a Ph.D. from Harvard University and leader of the Niagara Movement, which helped give birth to the National Association for the Advancement of Colored People, had died.

It was also upon this day in 1963 that the March on Washington for Jobs and Freedom was held in Washington, D.C. An estimated crowd of 250,000 to 300,000 people came by foot, car, bus, train, and plane to bear witness to the injustices of the nation and to advocate for civil and economic rights for all Black Americans. Ten speakers—unfortunately, all men—arose to speak from the platform erected before the Lincoln Memorial. The final address proved to be the most memorable, and it has gone down in history as one of the greatest speeches ever delivered, a speech considered by many to be the greatest speech of the twentieth century.

At age thirty-four, the Reverend Dr. Martin Luther King Jr. delivered what is now known as his "I Have a Dream" speech. The most famous excerpts of the speech were delivered at the prompting of iconic Gospel singer Mahalia Jackson. Seated on the platform with Dr. King, and sensing the weariness of his audience, who had spent the afternoon listening to speech after speech in the August sun, Jackson cried out, "Tell them about the dream, Martin." At that point, in a move that only could have been inspired by the Holy Spirit, Dr. King set aside his prepared speech and spoke of his dream.

The "Dream" speech was a ready oratorical flourish for Dr. King, one Jackson had heard in previous speeches, including one he had delivered at the Great March for Freedom in Detroit on June 23, 1963. Historians note that it was a borrowed flourish from the Reverend Dr. Prathia Hall, a twenty-three-year-old preaching Black woman who used it while offering a speech at the charred remains of the Mount Olive Baptist Church in 1962, which had been torched by the local Ku Klux Klan.

We know the words of this speech and the images conveyed by it quite well. It is a part of our collective memory and our national lexicon. Dr. King said,

> And so even though we face the difficulties of today and tomorrow, I still have a dream. It is a dream deeply rooted in the American dream. I have a dream that one day this nation will rise up and live out the true meaning of its creed: "We hold these truths to be self-evident, that all men are created equal." I have a dream that one day on the red hills of Georgia, the sons of former slaves and the sons of former slave owners will be able to sit down together at the table of brotherhood. I have a dream that one day even the state of Mississippi, a state sweltering with the heat of injustice, sweltering with the heat of oppression, will be transformed into an oasis of freedom and justice. I have a dream that my four little children will one day live in a nation where they will not be judged by the color of their skin but by the content of their character. I have a *dream* today!

Still, we would do well to remember that this was not Dr. King's dream in totality. This is the dream that we tell, the dream we find palpable, the dream that uplifts us and gives us feelings of euphoria. This is the part of Dr. King's dream that we can tolerate, for it is a dream that does not come with demands.

However, Dr. King's larger dream was radical, one most people would deny came from the mouth and pen of Martin King because of its searing and demanding tone. Dr. King did not just call for shared lunches between the descendants of slaves and slave owners. No, Dr. King called for a "Bill of Rights for the Disadvantaged," akin the to the GI Bill of Rights, a bill with which "the full resources of the society would be used to attack the tenacious poverty which so paradoxically exists in the midst of plenty."

Dr. King did not simply call for an oasis of freedom, he also called for a guaranteed income—not minimum wage, but a living wage for all Americans. He also called on America to cancel all debts owed by impoverished foreign governments to alleviate the strain of poverty upon the people of those nations.

Dr. King called for countering the tripartite, unbridled evils of capitalism, militarism, and racism. He chose the right text, Isaiah 40:4–5: "every valley shall be exalted, and every hill and mountain shall be made low, the rough places will be made plain, and the crooked places will be made straight; and the glory of the Lord shall be revealed and all flesh shall see it together."

Why We Can't Wait ... to Tear Down Confederate Monuments

(An editorial published in the *Dallas Morning News* on September 2, 2017.)

Fifty-four springs ago, the Reverend Martin Luther King languished for eight days in solitary confinement in a Birmingham jail in Alabama. His crime? Not waiting another moment for justice.

As he remained imprisoned, eight distinguished Birmingham clergymen penned an open letter indirectly to Dr. King, which they published in the local paper. The letter criticized the unwavering demands for justice being pursued in the city. They wrote, "*Responsible* [emphasis mine] citizens have undertaken to work on various problems which cause racial friction and unrest ... We recognize the natural impatience of people who feel that their hopes are slow in being realized. But we are convinced that these demonstrations are unwise and untimely ... All of us need to face that responsibility and find *proper channels* [emphasis mine] for its accomplishment."[44]

In response to their indirect indictment of his mission and work, Dr. King penned his own letter, first around the borders of a copy of the paper condemning him, then upon scraps of paper smuggled to him by a Black trustee. What resulted has been called one of the greatest treatises on nonviolent direct action in human history: the aptly titled "Letter from Birmingham Jail." The letter is filled with what have become some of Dr. King's most powerful and cherished quotes. Dr. King masterfully countered his criticizers' calls for a slowed path to justice by stressing the urgency of justice *now*.

He wrote, "For years now I have heard the word 'Wait!' It rings in the ear of every Negro with piercing familiarity. This 'Wait' has almost always meant 'Never.' We must come to see, with one of our distinguished jurists, that 'justice too long delayed is justice denied.'"

This summer, I revisited Dr. King's letter and the book in which it is included as a chapter, *Why We Can't Wait*. I read the book as a part of my family's participation in Mayor Mike Rawlings' phenomenal summer reading program to encourage literacy in our city. Now, given the unnecessary delays and deflections of expeditious removal of Confederate monuments in Dallas by the mayor and by some members of the Dallas City Council—delays and deflections supported by some opinion writers at this very paper—I feel it is important that I offer a brief summary of what Dr. King taught me.

What I learned from Dr. King is that even well-intentioned people can delay justice by supporting bureaucratic processes aimed at keeping the peace. Dr. King said, "True peace is not merely the absence of tension; it is the presence of justice." Unfortunately, the present efforts of the mayor maintain a falsified peace.

Mayor Rawlings and the majority of the Dallas City Council have already stated it would be an injustice for Confederate monuments to remain erect in public spaces. Usually, when a clear majority is present on an issue before the council, a vote is called. Instead, the mayor has called for and created a task force. In calling for and creating a task force on Confederate monuments, our well-intentioned mayor has conspired to continue to promote injustice in Dallas. For every single second that these monuments remain in public view, injustice is being done to the citizens of Dallas, especially communities that have long suffered under the blunt force of white supremacy.

And other well-intentioned people, such as the *Dallas Morning News*'s James Ragland, who has called for "a calm, comprehensive, and deliberate approach to dismantling the Confederacy legacy," serve as accomplices in this injustice.

What is needed to tear down Confederate monuments in Dallas is not more time or talk, but rather courage.

Dr. King had some good words on this too: "The ultimate measure of a [person] is not where [she or he] stands in moments of comfort and convenience, but where [she or he] stands at times of challenge and controversy." He also said, "The time is always ripe to do right."

I implore Mayor Rawlings and the Dallas City Council to do what is right. Do not push off justice for another day. Call for a vote to remove all Confederate monuments without delay.

All you need is the moral courage to do so.

The Fire This Time

(An editorial published in the *Dallas Morning News* under the title "Sins of Slavery Still Haunt US" on August 30, 2019.)

"To be [Black] in this country and to be relatively conscious is to be in a rage almost all the time." —James Baldwin

Last August, deep in the East Texas woods, I sat at a table with my wife's great-aunt Cleo, who had traveled hundreds of miles from the Bay Area for our family's fiftieth reunion. A sharp, spry, and still strikingly beautiful woman of eighty-eight, the former baby of the family now sat in her full glory as our matriarch. I am still not sure what triggered her sudden recollection, but while seated at that table, Aunt Cleo began to tell me about the last time her great-grandmother Mittie's mother, Aunt Cleo's great-great-grandmother, saw her own mother alive. Great-great-grandmother's last recollection of her mother was seeing her seated on a tree stump weeping hysterically as she was being sold to another slave owner.

A few years ago, Mittie's mother's story, though painful, could have been received with some emotional and psychological distance, void of any present-day emotional touchpoints for most Americans. This is no longer the case. The tears of Mississippi children whose parents were suddenly taken away from them in an ICE roundup prove otherwise. Today, other children lie in cages, wrapped in foil blankets soiled by their own waste, placed there by a US government that has admitted it cannot guarantee that these children will ever see their own parents again.

August 2019 marks four hundred years since twenty West Africans arrived upon these shores after being stolen from their families, never to see them again. Summer 2019 marks the one hundredth year since the Red Summer of 1919 in Omaha, a reign of white supremacist terror that extended from late winter to early autumn. Racial violence raged in more than three dozen American cities and one rural county, resulting in hundreds of deaths. Among the more brutal was that of Will Brown, a Black man lynched and whose corpse was fired upon hundreds of times before being cut down, tied, and dragged behind an automobile before ultimately being doused with oil and set ablaze. Afterward, bits of Brown's charred body were sold as souvenirs throughout the streets of Omaha.

August 2019 also marks just five years since another Black man named Brown—a Black teenager named Michael Brown—was fatally shot six times by Ferguson police officer Darren Wilson, a tragedy that launched the Black Lives Matter movement further into the public consciousness. Five years later, a witness to the shooting still alleges that Brown was shot with his hands up. Often forgotten is that a crowdfunding campaign for Wilson received an outpouring of financial support from white supremacists.

We live in a time when police are frequently called when Black people engage in such mundane activities as meeting at Starbucks, entering their own homes, and cashing their paychecks at banks, a time when a young white supremacist from Allen, Texas, can travel six hundred fifty miles to kill Brown people who were shopping for school supplies with their kids. There is a sense that our nation has rapidly reverted to a more frequent and public racist disposition, one that some mistakenly thought was left behind decades ago.

Frequently, it appears that one important influence on this resurgence is the present occupant of 1600 Pennsylvania Avenue in Washington, D.C., during whose campaign and presidency hate groups have flourished to a record high in America, according to the Southern Poverty Law Center—a 30-percent increase over the last four years. Tweets that degrade cities and countries where the population is majority Black or that refer to Latinx people as rapists only solidify white supremacist inclinations.

Recently, when I picked up my children from school, our second-born raced into the car with a burning question, one that she and her classmates must have been entertaining for the day. "Dad," she said, "Is Donald Trump going to send us back to slavery?"

My response was swift and strong "no!"

In retrospect, the question deserved more authentic engagement. If nothing else, her question revealed a keen sensibility to our current climate in which the distance has narrowed between Mittie's mother being snatched from her mother's arms and Mississippi children being snatched from their mothers' arms. We live in an era when the fire of racial terror burns anew.

It is time to reconsider how far we have come.

An Empty Warrior

(Delivered September 28, 2019, in Toronto, Ontario, Canada, for the Fundraising Gala for the Indigenous Water Initiative,)

The opening scenes of the 2001 American cinematic masterpiece *Ali* starring Black American actor Will Smith depicts a young Cassius Marcellus Clay Jr. as he is boarding public transportation in his hometown of Louisville, Kentucky, early in September of 1955. Cassius would have been thirteen years old. As he is guided by his father's hand to the back of the bus, a sign appears overhead. It reads "For Coloreds Only."

Young Cassius then sets his gaze upon the front page of the daily newspaper being read all around him. What he sees gives him pause. Adorning those pages is the mutilated corpse of a young fourteen-year-old Chicago boy named Emmett Till.

On August 28, 1955, young Emmett had been kidnapped under the cover of night, driven over seventy miles across the state of Mississippi, tortured by multiple groups of adult men at multiple locations, and shot dead before having his body affixed to a cotton gin with barbed wire and discarded as rubbish into the Black Bayou in Glendora, Mississippi. Imam Suleiman and I traveled together with our families last year to the final place of Emmett Till's torture and ultimate demise. I traveled back this past February to the very place his submerged body was brought back to shore three days later.

Emmett Till had been accused of harassing a white woman in America's Jim Crow South, an act that, according to the unwritten laws of Jim Crow, was deserving of death. Just last year, that same woman, Carolyn Bryant Donham, now eighty-five years old, revealed that she fabricated the entire story that inspired her husband and brother-in-law's heinous act. Still, despite her admission of her role in young Emmett's murder, she remains free.

This brutal and tortuous context does not even address the place of Cassius' birth: Louisville, Kentucky. As I wrote in my book *Stakes Is High: Race, Faith, and Hope for America* regarding what would ultimately become Cassius' monumental life, during America's antebellum period, Kentucky was a Northern-border slave state. Louisville itself was home to a major US slave market. From Louisville, first upon the Ohio River, then down the Mississippi River, human captives were shipped southward to be sold or delivered to the highest bidder. After the American Civil War, Kentucky remained home to heinous acts of racial intimidation. Whippings, shootings, and lynching accompanied the rise of numerous Ku Klux Klan chapters across the state.

Cassius was born on January 17, 1942, one month after America entered World War II following Japan's bombing of Pearl Harbor. It was in this same year that Nazi Germany enacted its Final Solution and began herding Jewish people to concentration camps to engage in a systematic program of genocide that would take 6 million lives. It was in this same year that the Congress for Racial Equality was founded by pacifists in Chicago and began to use nonviolent tactics to oppose segregation, providing the blueprint for what would become the American civil rights movement.

It is imperative that the life of Cassius Clày be placed in this social context. Cassius Clay was born into a context of war. He was born into a context of rabid racism and racial discrimination. And he was born into a context of the reemergence of a radical opposition to violence, racial or otherwise. These are the realities that first watered Clay's soil.

Black Americans faithfully served American forces in World War II as they had faithfully served in every American war. Their courageous efforts helped to liberate millions across the world, but their efforts in seeking to liberate their own people from the white supremacy they faced at home proved futile. When Black Americans returned home from war, many were brutally attacked while wearing their military uniforms. An attack on decorated Black army veteran Isaac Woodard on February 12,

1946, while he was still in uniform by South Carolina police left Mr. Woodard blinded for the rest of his life. He died at age seventy-three in 1992. J. C. Farmer, a nineteen-year-old veteran, was lynched by a mob of twenty white men in North Carolina on August 3, 1946, shot down by submachine guns as his own mother watched in horror.

These atrocities and many more, experienced as Black American serviceman returned home, further fanned the flames of resistance in the Black community. These fires of resistance, too, found fertile ground in Clay's young heart. As the story has been told, we first bear witness to the flames of resistance to injustice manifest in young Clay after he has the tragic juvenile experience of having his bicycle stolen. Enraged, young Clay was ready to fight. Thankfully, he encountered someone who knew how to hone and direct his aggression.

Cassius began training as an amateur boxer, developing both skill and discipline. He won many amateur bouts and later qualified for the Olympics. He represented America in 1960 in Rome during a time when Black Americans were still being routinely lynched, still being denied integration through public accommodation, and still being denied the right to vote. Cassius emerged victorious in these Olympics, earning gold in the light heavyweight division and entering the professional ranks later that year.

Now, I have studied the etymology of Cassius Marcellus' name. And, I can assure you, Cassius Clay was aptly named. And not just because he was named after his father who himself was named after Cassius Marcellus Clay, the nineteenth-century politician and abolitionist from the state of Kentucky where Jr. was born, who freed the slaves that were handed down as his inheritance from his father and paid those who decided to stay wages for their work.

Interestingly enough, it is an old Roman name with an uncertain meaning. However, some etymologists offer that it is possibly derived from the Latin *cassus* meaning "hollow" or "empty." Marcellus is also a Latin name. It has some association with the Roman god of war named Mars. Some list its meaning as "hammer." Others list its meaning as "warrior." Either way, I believe that Cassius Clay was aptly named. He was, in fact, an empty warrior.

Now, I am in no way degrading Cassius Clay. As a matter of fact, I believe we should all aspire to be empty warriors. For me, an empty warrior is a fighter standing ready to be filled by God with a greater purpose. Today, the world celebrates Cassius Clay for what he ultimately became. But he would not have become what he ultimately became without being born into this context and walking this path.

Yes, we should aspire to be empty warriors, for we too have been born and now bear witness to a global context of rabid racism, hatred, and injustice. White supremacy still rages across the globe. Earlier this month, I stood and spoke for a memorial outside a Walmart in El Paso, Texas, where a young white supremacist drove ten hours and six hundred fifty miles to kill twenty-two people because of their Brown skin. Earlier this week, I stood outside the courthouse for the beginnings of yet another trial of a white police officer who shot an unarmed Black man, this one named Botham Jean, this one shot for the crime of being in his own home.

More people are displaced from their homes by war and strife than at any other point in American history. Poverty is growing, and communities from Flint, Michigan, to the Indigenous people of this land are still without clean drinking water.

And so, in the midst of all these horrors and atrocities and many more, we can resign ourselves to sit on the sidelines of history, or we can empty ourselves of pride, selfishness, and self-preservation that we might be filled by God with just pursuits.

I praise God for the example of Cassius Clay! Let us take our righteous indignation of injustice and hone it through discipline and skill, and let us sacrifice our very bodies in the cause of justice, knowing that together we can claim victory!

For I still believe that the moral arc of the universe is long, but it bends toward justice!

I still believe weeping may endure for a night, but joy comes in the morning!

I still believe if God be for us, who can be against us?

Who here tonight is ready to stand for peace?

Who here tonight is ready to stand for truth?

Who here tonight is ready to stand for righteousness?

Who here tonight is ready to stand for justice?

Who tonight is ready to give to make this world a better place for our children and for generations unborn?

Who here tonight believes that together, we can change the world?

Well, let's continue to stand, let's continue to work, let's continue to fight, let's continue to give until justice flows like water, and righteousness like a mighty stream!

Thank God for African Angels!
Exodus 12:21-23

(Delivered November 8, 2020, in Dallas, Texas, the day following
Joseph R. Biden's election as the forty-sixth President of
the United States of America.)

This week, Americans received a rare introduction to
angelology.

Yes, angelology. This is a thing.

Angelology is the study or doctrine of angels. It is considered
one of the major components of systematic theology, in which
Dr. King received his doctorate of philosophy from Boston
University in 1955. Systematic theology seeks to "arrange
religious truths in a self-consistent whole."

Last week, during a streamed prayer service, President
Donald Trump's spiritual advisor Pastor Paula White—a one-
time protégé of Bishop T. D. Jakes who has fallen out of favor
with him in recent years—prayed against so-called "demonic
confederacies" seeking to steal the presidential election from
Trump, a claim that has proven to be unfounded.

As a part of her earnest prayer, Pastor White presented her
views on angelology as she called upon angels from Africa to
come to America and engage in spiritual warfare so that Donald
Trump would emerge victorious in his reelection bid as the
President of the United States. She declared that these African
angels would strike down Trump's opponents. She then declared
victory for his campaign. Clearly, her petitions failed to deliver
her desired result, but her performance of these petitions has
now become a fixture in popular culture, including in mockery
across social media.

Biblically speaking, angels are best known as messengers of
God. That is what angel, or *angelos*, means in Greek. Angels come
to deliver messages from God to humanity.

In the book of Genesis, angels deliver a message to Abram that he and his wife Sarai will bear a child despite their advanced age and history of infertility. An angel appears to Zechariah and tells him to name his unborn son John. This son would come as a forerunner to Christ. Angels appear to shepherds tending their flock at night to inform them of the birth of Jesus Christ.

Biblically speaking, we also witness that some angels are connected to countries and territories. In the book of Daniel, the prophet fasts and prays for twenty-one days to receive an answer from God. An angel ultimately appears to Daniel with a message, but first the angel informs Daniel that as soon as he began praying, the angel was sent by God. However, for the past twenty-one days, the angel had been in an epic battle with the "prince of Persia," in this case a demonic force. Only after the archangel Michael came to engage in the battle was the angel released to carry his message to Daniel.

Angels fight, biblically speaking. They engage in battle against the enemies of God and God's people so that the plan of God continues to be accomplished. In Revelation 12:7–10, the Bible says, "Then war broke out in heaven. Michael and his angels fought against the dragon and the dragon and his angels fought back. But he was not strong enough, and they lost their place in heaven. The great dragon was hurled down—that ancient serpent called the devil, or Satan, who leads the whole world astray. He was hurled to the earth, and his angels with him."

When angels come, they show up with a divine message. When angels come, they appear in a specific territory. When angels come, they arrive to fight against the enemies of God and God's people.

So, I decided to engage Pastor Paula White's prayerful petition. If African angels were to come to America, what would they say? What would they do? I decided that the best way to find an answer to my inquiry was to bear witness to what "African" angels have already done.

In the book of Exodus, Israel is in bondage in Egypt, subject to an evil leader called Pharaoh. Under Pharaoh, Israel has suffered a multiplicity of brutalities. Intimidated by their growing number and strength, the pharaoh conspires to limit their power, their voice, and their influence in the nation. I think the pharaoh was concerned about losing his power, and, if Egypt had had a democracy like ours, I am sure that the pharaoh would have worried about new congressional districts being created by this growth, fearful about new voters entering the electorate.

So, the Pharaoh said, "Look, the people of Israel now outnumber us and are stronger than we are. We must make a plan to keep them from growing even more."[45] I am sure that the pharaoh suggested that Egyptian envoys gerrymander congressional districts in their favor. I am sure that the pharaoh encouraged the passage of voter ID laws to shut out Israelite voters from the polls. I am sure that the pharaoh decided to limit ballot drop boxes to one per county. I am sure that the pharaoh decided to eliminate polling locations so that Israelites had to wait in long lines to vote. Yes, I am sure that Pharaoh decided to deny returning citizens the opportunity to vote if they had not paid all their fees, a new poll tax. I am sure that the Egyptian poll workers told the Israelites that their Israelite Lives Matter shirts were a political statement and were not allowed in the polling location.

The Bible says that Egypt became ruthless in their dealings with Israel. "They appointed brutal slave drivers over them, hoping to wear them down with crushing labor. They forced them to build cities as supply centers for the king. They worked the people of Israel without mercy. They made their lives bitter, forcing them to mix mortar and make bricks and do all the work in the fields."[46] They denied them universal healthcare. They refused to pass an appropriate stimulus bill amid a pandemic to help these essential workers. They gutted the Voting Rights Act. They implemented deregulation to allow big businesses to pollute their communities and the earth. They refused to pay workers a guaranteed minimum income.

But somehow, the Bible says, that the more they were brutalized, the more they were oppressed, the more they were terrorized, the more they were maligned—the more they continued to grow. Yes, the more they were pushed down, the more powerful they became. And when they cried out to God, God raised a leader named Moses to take them out of Egypt's bondage.

As part of God's strategy for their liberation, we are introduced to some African angels. In Exodus 12, Israel is instructed by Moses to "Go, pick out a lamb or young goat for each of your families, and slaughter the Passover animal. Drain the blood into a basin. Then take a bundle of hyssop branches and dip it into the blood. Then brush the hyssop across the top and sides of the doorframe of your houses. And no one may go out through the door until the morning. For the LORD will pass through the land to strike down the Egyptians. But when he sees the blood on the top and sides of the doorframe, the LORD will pass over your home. He will not permit the death angel to enter your house and strike you down!"[47]

When I look upon the witness of these angels in Egypt, these African angels, I see that when the angels came, they came to punish the wicked. When they came, they showed up to liberate the oppressed. When the African angels came, they arrived to illuminate a message from God that those covered by the Blood of the Lamb, by the grace and mercy of God, would be passed over.

I thank God for African angels! They are angels who hold the wicked accountable for evil. They are angels who come to challenge systems of marginalization, oppression, and suppression to liberate God's people. African angels come to illuminate God's message of grace, mercy, and divine protection.

Pastor Paula did not have to pray for African angels! All she needed to do was look back through the corridors of history to discover that African angels are already here. As the writer of the book of Hebrews penned, "Therefore, since we are surrounded by such a huge crowd of witnesses to the life of faith, let us strip off every weight that slows us down."[48]

I am so grateful that we are, in fact, surrounded by a great cloud of witnesses—African angels—witnesses to the life of faith, who stood up against evil, who worked to liberate the oppressed, and who came to bring us a message of God's grace, mercy, and divine protection.

I thank God for African angels!
John Lewis is an African angel!
Amelia Boynton Robinson is an African angel!
Fannie Lou Hamer is an African angel!
Ida B. Wells is an African angel!
Rosa Parks is an African angel!
Richard Allen is an African angel!
Sojourner Truth is an African angel!
Malcolm X is an African angel!
Harriet Tubman is an African angel!
Shirley Chisholm is an African angel!

My papa, Bishop W. Williams, who faced down the KKK and went on to be elected a county commissioner and a county judge, is an African angel!

Denise McNair, Carole Robertson, Addie Mae Collins, and Cynthia Wesley—four little girls who were bombed into eternity in 1963 and whose deaths wrought the Civil Rights Act of 1964—are African angels!

Clementa C. Pinckney, Cynthia Marie Graham-Hurd, Susie. Jackson, Ethel Lee Lance, DePayne Middleton-Doctor, Tywanza Sanders, Daniel L. Simmons, Sharonda Coleman-Singleton, and Myra Thompson—the nine faithful who were shot down at a Bible study at Charleston's Mother Emanuel AME Church—are African angels! Their deaths brought down the Confederate flag in South Carolina and Confederate monuments across the country,

Botham Jean is an African angel!
Atatiana Jefferson is an African angel!
Elijah McClain is an African angel!
Ahmaud Arbery is an African angel!
Breonna Taylor is an African angel!
George Floyd is an African angel!

And these angels tell us to keep pressing on, to keep fighting on, and to not grow weary in good-doing. It's been a long time coming, but change will surely come!

Conclusion: Can a Virus Heal America?

On January 4, 2020, my family and I joined Dr. Brian Williams and his family for lunch in Dallas. A Black military veteran and Harvard-trained surgeon, Dr. Williams rose to national prominence for his courageous words on race in America following the deadly ambush of five Dallas police officers after a peaceful rally and march on July 7, 2016. At the time, he was a surgeon at Dallas' Parkland Hospital, which received most of the wounded. He personally operated on the officers and had the grim responsibility of pronouncing some dead. We were united in this tragedy as I had been a featured speaker at the rally. I ultimately served as a marshal for the impromptu march that followed, and I offered a benediction and instructions for disbursing minutes before tragedy struck.

Dr. Williams, now an associate professor of trauma and acute care surgery at the University of Chicago, spoke with me about a commentary for the *Chicago Tribune* that he was writing about race disparity in healthcare with the hopes of having it published in time for the upcoming Martin Luther King Jr. national holiday. He extended to me an opportunity to coauthor this commentary, and I readily accepted. In both Chicago and Dallas, recent reports on disparities in life expectancy among different races had been released. Chicago ranked highest in America, with an alarming thirty-year gap. In Dallas, while only five miles separated them geographically, twenty-four years separated the highest and lowest life expectancies by zip code. In our commentary, we noted the words of Dr. King, who had prominently stated at a medical conference in Chicago in 1966 that "of all the forms of inequality, injustice in health is the most shocking and the most inhumane because it often results in physical death." Our commentary was well received and became the foundation for remarks offered by the medical school's dean during his annual MLK address.

I had prepared myself for frequent odysseys in 2020 as experienced in 2019, and early 2020 provided without any hints of anything otherwise. That January, I spent several days in Iowa leading up to their presidential primary and included a stop in Denver as well with Vote Common Good. To end the month, I spoke on a panel hosted by the Smithsonian National Museum of African American History and Culture concerning the future of the Black Church in America. The following week, I traveled to Washington, D.C. with my wife, Yulise, to attend an emergency meeting of the National Black Leadership Summit of the Congressional Black Caucus. It was quite a time to be back in D.C., as the summit was being held simultaneously with the impeachment hearing and Senate vote on President Trump. While we were still in D.C., President Trump offered his State of the Union address. Before we went out for dinner that evening, we were advised that some of the roads would be blocked off due to the president's motorcade.

One of the featured speakers at the summit is the indomitable Bishop William J. Barber II, whom I had first met in his home state of North Carolina when we both served as speakers for the Wild Goose Festival during the summer of 2017. In January of 2018, I had the honor of hosting him at our church in Dallas for a clergy training as he relaunched the Poor People's Campaign. In his remarks, Bishop Barber poignantly compared the impeachment proceedings to the horrid legacy of Southern justice which repeatedly conspired to cover up crimes against Black humanity, stating, "This was the everyday practice of Southern justice under Jim Crow, and [Senator] McConnell has brought Southern justice again to the United States Senate."

Before we departed from D.C., I accompanied my wife, an attorney who works in transformative justice and co-founder of the first alternative to incarceration program for emerging adults in Texas history, to visit a group of men incarcerated as youths and given life sentences. As in my previous visits to prisons, I was overwhelmed by the overrepresentation of Black and Brown bodies there. I joined with them in a brief circle of dialogue about their hopes for reform in the criminal legal system. Before departing, I attempted to offer them words of hope and encouragement despite their experiences in a system that disproportionately locks up Black and Brown youth and throws away the keys.

While at the jail, I learned that the cemetery adjacent to the prison was the final resting place of J. Edgar Hoover, the notorious, long-tenured head of the Federal Bureau of Investigation. Hoover terrorized a vast number of people and communities during his lengthy stranglehold over the agency, including Black Americans and civil rights workers. Under Hoover's leadership, the Counter Intelligence Program (COINTELPRO) was initiated; its stated goals were to "expose, disrupt, misdirect, discredit, or otherwise *neutralize* the activities of Black nationalists," as well as to the stop the rise of a so-called "Black messiah" such as Dr. Martin Luther King Jr.

The late, renowned historian Dr. John Henrik Clarke once stated, "History is a clock that people use to tell their political and cultural time of day. It is a compass they use to find themselves on the map of human geography. It tells them where they are, but more importantly, what they must be."[49] Indeed, this history spoke loudly to me. We must be better; we must become better as a nation. And we can only hope to be better by taking a clear eye to history and acknowledging how white supremist ideals and policies such as Hoover's helped set the stage for our present era of mass incarceration in America. Then we must have the collective courage necessary to dismantle this system and erect something more just in its place.

After returning to Dallas, a few days later I departed from Dallas to lead another civil rights pilgrimage through the Deep South. During our stop in Birmingham that February, we had the honor of meeting Sarah Collins Rudolph. I had met Mrs. Rudolph's sister, Junie Collins Williams, several years prior when she spoke in Dallas. I was so impacted by her words that they became the inspiration for the first chapter of my first book in 2014.

Known as the "fifth little girl," twelve-year-old Sarah Collins had stood in the threshold of the women's lounge on the bottom level of the Sixteenth Street Baptist Church in Birmingham on the morning of September 15, 1963. As we sat together, she offered her final remembrances of her sister, Addie Mae Collins (fourteen), along with Cynthia Wesley (fourteen), Carole Robertson (fourteen), and Denise McNair (eleven). She recalled standing at the door watching the girls tie one another's sashes as they prepared to head upstairs to the sanctuary and help lead Sunday worship.

Then everything went black.

As young Sarah regained consciousness, she called for Addie Mae but received no response. Her older sister was dead. The blast had decapitated her. She was later identified by just the shoes on her feet. The other three girls were also dead. The powerful blast had disrobed them all. The girls were innocent victims of a vicious act of racial violence devised and perpetrated by the Ku Klux Klan, one that would forever change our nation and the civil rights movement.

I sat on Mrs. Rudolph's right side, listening intently as she spoke to us. But as she continued to speak, I began to focus in on the faded yet visible scars that framed the socket of the right eye that she lost in the blast. Those scars impacted me as much as the faded blood stains still visible under the carport of Medgar Evers' home in Jackson, Mississippi, a visceral reminder of the amount of bloodshed that has accompanied our odyssey to freedom.

Still in our nation today are many people who still bear the physical scars of white supremacy. Our encounter was a sobering yet spiritual experience. My heart broke for Mrs. Rudolph as she later shared that in addition to her injuries, at the time, she had not received any formal apology from the state of Alabama. Nor had she or her family received any financial compensation for their pain and suffering. Quite frequently, she felt forgotten, even at times in Birmingham. I could not help but wonder how many others who have sacrificed and lost so much amid this struggle likewise feel forgotten.

We must never forget!

During our February travels through the Deep South, I began to also listen more intently to increasing daily reports of a new virus that was spreading rapidly across the globe. As I listened, I began to take greater precautions, frequently washing and sanitizing my hands while fighting the urge to place my hands on my face. The virus still seemed at once distant but near as infections began to rise in the Pacific Northwest. Not many days passed after our return to Dallas before there were reports of the first infections in North Texas.

I quickly made the decision to suspend all in-person gatherings of our congregation and to bring our children home from school to continue their studies there. Shortly thereafter, my wife began to work remotely from home. During these early moments of the coronavirus pandemic, I was made intimately aware of the privileges that enabled our family to make such immediate transitions back home. I was also intimately aware of the many families in my church and community who were without such privileges. I immediately worked to create an emergency relief fund through our church to provide support to individuals and families who were certain to experience financial challenges. By the grace of God, many people responded generously to this initiative, and we were able to provide grants to families and individuals directly impacted by COVID-19 and to people needing financial assistance for food, housing, prescriptions, co-pays, and other critical needs. We also formed partnerships that enabled our congregation to provide free packets of personal protective equipment and hand sanitizer to our church and community.

Just as I had done in those early moments of our renewed struggle to bring down Confederate monuments in Dallas in July 2017, I took to social media with a flurry of posts. I was convinced that gathering people together for worship inside a building was one of the worst choices that could be made amid the pandemic. One responder to an early post offered what quickly became my mantra for these uncertain times: "Love looks like an empty building." These proclamations did not sit well with some others, including some clergy. My remarks were soon criticized via public posts and private direct messages. However, not long after receiving such criticism, reports emerged of multiple deaths and infections in communities across the country connected to in-person worship gatherings.

Another result of my outspokenness was that I began to receive calls from local and national media to offer commentary on the coronavirus and its impacts. For one publication, I was asked to offer a prayer for where we could find hope during this harrowing time. I also posed while seated in our empty sanctuary for a socially distanced photo shoot for a journalist who was documenting life amid COVID-19. In each interview, I offered that I expected the virus to further exploit and expose the racial and economic fissures long present within our nation, evidence of something in the water that has haunted us for generations. I also noted that I expected the virus to have an undue impact on Black, Brown, and Indigenous people, as well as on the poor. Repeatedly, I expressed particular concern for Dallas, the county seat of the largest uninsured workforce in America, as well as for South and Southern Dallas, the epicenter of big-city poverty in America.

Still, in the face of these anticipated happenings, I began to wonder if the coronavirus had the capacity to heal America. I began to contemplate whether the shared harms of the pandemic, with its lack of respect for personhood, would cause the people of our nation to finally rise up and root out the toxic pollutant of white supremacy that has infected America's waters since its inception. Having written about racial health disparities with Dr. Williams to begin the year, I pondered whether a virus— one that has already proven its capacity to bring harm to the rich and to the poor alike, to cities, suburbs, and rural communities alike, to people of every race, ethnicity, and creed, would reveal to us what Dr. King had penned while captive in a Birmingham jail: "Injustice anywhere is a threat to justice everywhere. We are caught in an inescapable network of mutuality, tied in a single garment of destiny. Whatever affects one directly, affects all indirectly."

Suddenly, ideals such as universal healthcare, guaranteed income, student debt cancellation, and other equity-granting measures did not seem to be handouts so much as necessary correctives to historic harms and oppressive systems. Suddenly, earned paid sick leave for all made sense for all. Suddenly, access to quality foods and shelter became a concern for all as industries and businesses ground to a halt and as families for the first time in their lives found themselves waiting in long lines in luxury cars at food pantries. I pondered if empathy amid the pandemic could emerge as a great equalizer and create renewed opportunities for policy-based healing in America.

Yet, as the spring progressed, so did a renewed and disturbing drumbeat—Black lives felled to white supremacist violence and police brutality. News emerged of an unarmed twenty-five-year-old Black jogger near Brunswick, Georgia, who had been pursued by white men in vehicles and trapped like game on February 23. The men shot and killed Ahmaud Arbery, claiming that they believed he posed a threat to them and to their community.

The next report came from Louisville, Kentucky. An unarmed twenty-six-year-old Black woman was killed by police on March 13 while sleeping in her own apartment. Police had obtained a no-knock warrant to enter the home of Breonna Taylor, a local first responder, because they believed she was facilitating the drug-dealing activities of her former boyfriend. No evidence was found to support these claims.

Amid these deaths came news of a false accusation that easily could have resulted in the death of another Black man. Harvard graduate and avid birder Christian Cooper was falsely accused of threatening the life of Amy Cooper (no relation), a white woman, after requesting that she place her dog on a leash (as required by law) while at a designated section of Central Park. Her tearful pleas for police would have easily resulted in Christian Cooper's lynching a few generations earlier.

Suddenly, it felt as though we were facing two pandemics—the coronavirus and white supremacy—each vying for supremacy over the other while simultaneously conspiring to together wreak as much havoc on our nation as possible.

In late May, I came across an article regarding the ninety-ninth anniversary of the 1921 Tulsa, Oklahoma, massacre that May. In the most gruesome act of racial violence in American history, over three hundred Black people were killed over the course of forty-eight hours of white supremacist violence. This massacre holds the dubious distinction of being the first time that bombs were dropped on American citizens on American soil, as kerosene bombs were dropped from airplanes overhead on Black Tulsa's Greenwood District, known fondly as "Black Wall Street," a center of Black economic progress, entrepreneurship, and wealth. The Greenwood District is located a mile from the winding Arkansas River that flows east to southeast through four states. In the state of Arkansas, the Arkansas River Valley was the frequent site of Black lynching and night rides by the Ku Klux Klan, and the areas around the southern boundaries of the river valley were deemed sundown towns where it was illegal to be present as a Black person after dark. During the summer of 1965, a young Black man was tied to a tree and brutally whipped by members of the Klan for violating that rule near Booneville, Arkansas. According to the Encyclopedia of Arkansas, by 1970, when sundown towns were at their peak, half of all incorporated communities outside the traditional South excluded Black people.

There's something in the water.

In that moment, I could not help but think about how proximate this history remains to us today. Indeed, in Tulsa, they are still uncovering new mass graves from the massacre. By placing the Tulsa massacre in its historical context, a mirror is lifted to us in present day.

In 1921 in America, the massive number of Black casualties resulting from white supremacy was not the only crisis that was raging in the nation. The world was just coming out of the Spanish flu pandemic, which claimed close to 100 million lives, including those of five hundred thousand Americans. During this time, the Ku Klux Klan was experiencing a resurgence, growing to nearly 8 million members strong and dominating both local and state elections from Portland, Maine, to Portland, Oregon. Klan members controlled the state governments of Colorado and Indiana. White supremacist president Woodrow Wilson oversaw the resegregation of multiple agencies of the federal government, including the Treasury Department and the US Postal Service. During the Wilson administration, in one instance, when it was impossible to segregate a Black man due to the nature of his work, a cage was built around him for him to perform his duties inside of.

Broken Black bodies in the streets. A lack of access to quality healthcare amid a pandemic. A resurgent political force steeped in white supremacy controlling many state governments. An unrepentant white supremacist president. Human beings put in cages. It could have easily been 2020. It was 2020.

Then the world stopped. For eight minutes and forty-six seconds we watched in collective horror as a Minneapolis police officer placed his knee to the neck of George Floyd, who was suspected of passing a counterfeit $20 bill while making a purchase. The officer's knee on Floyd's neck remained there two full minutes after Floyd was unconscious. That knee remained there for one whole minute after paramedics arrived. And, once again, through cell phone video footage, we were haunted by a Black man's call for help to his dearly departed mother and his repeated pleas for breath.

I can't breathe! Where have I heard that before? Eric Garner? Yes, but not just Eric Garner. That has been the plea of Black people throughout the expanse of our time upon these shores. This is the suffocating effect of white supremacy. And white supremacy comes with a body count.

The summer of 2020 gave us no less than the largest protest movement in American history, the Black Lives Matter movement. *The New York Times* offered that on June 6 alone, 500,000 people took to the streets in over 550 places across America. Overwhelmingly, these demonstrations were peaceful, with 93 percent of them declared so, according to the Armed Conflict Location and Event Data Project which analyzed over 7,750 Black Lives Matter demonstrations in all 50 states and Washington D.C. Demands to defund or abolish police departments—though far from being new demands—rose within the American consciousness and were debated by pundits and politicians alike.

Unfortunately, amid these uprisings against police brutality, more brutalities ensued. Some protestors were seriously injured by police. A few were killed. And the news of more incidents of police brutality—such as the strangling death of Elijah McClain in Aurora, Colorado, on August 24, 2019—gained national attention as the BLM movement continued to grow.

Rayshard Brooks, an unarmed twenty-seven-year-old Black man, was shot and killed in Atlanta, Georgia, on June 12, 2020, after he fell asleep in his car in the drive-through lane of a fast-food restaurant. Brooks was shot as he was running away from police officers. Later in the summer, we again watched in horror as an unarmed twenty-nine-year-old Black man named Jacob Blake was shot seven times in the back by a police officer in Kenosha, Wisconsin. Blake was shot on August 23 in front of his children, who were in the car. The shooting left Blake paralyzed. During the ensuing protests in Kenosha, a young, white seventeen-year-old from Illinois killed two unarmed protestors. He was hailed as an American hero by right-wing politicians and conservative media outlets, and over 2 million dollars were raised by private American citizens for his defense.

Amid all these brutalities, one long-fought battle was won in Dallas. The towering Confederate War Memorial in downtown Dallas was finally brought down in June. Although initially ensnarled in vigorous debate and opposition, and encumbered by litigation temporarily blocking its removal, it came down without much fanfare—a mere footnote, if that, to the perils that were facing our nation. However, for many of us who had been intimately engaged in this struggle, it was a glorious victory. I could not help but think that for the first time in 124 years in Dallas, Dallas children would be able to grow up in a city void of such grotesque celebrations of white supremacy. And I had long claimed that it would be impossible to achieve racial equity in the city if the city continued to cling to the myths of the Confederacy.

Also during the harrowing summer of 2020, I joined activists and faith leaders in issuing a list of ten demands following the uprisings in Dallas, across America, and around the globe in response to the lynching of George Floyd. In the list, formally titled "Ten New Directions for Public Safety and Positive Community Change," we proposed defunding police budgets and redirecting support to community initiatives. We also sought greater accountability for and transparency from police. These demands ultimately led to the formation of a fourteen-member working group in Dallas County. I was one of three faith leaders invited to serve on the group, and I was honored to join this assembly, composed of activists, police chiefs, and the city managers of most of the cities within Dallas County.

The working group met virtually over several weeks. We heard expert testimony and impact statements from victimized persons. After deliberating, we offered recommendations to the county regarding actions that should be taken. My wife Yulise offered compelling expert testimony on alternatives to incarceration programs that would save the county millions and dramatically decrease recidivism, all while keeping the largely Black and Brown young people of our most impoverished zip codes from becoming unnecessarily ensnarled within the criminal legal system. Although it is just a start, the Dallas County Commissioners Court voted to allocate $5 million to support several initiatives that the working group advocated for, including a mental health crisis center for the unhoused that would provide them needed support without taking them to jail. During the summer, the Dallas County Commissioners Court also passed a resolution that declared racism to be what it is: a public health emergency.

Soberingly, amid the summer's unprecedented national movement, elder leaders of the American civil rights movement began to depart from us. On the morning of July 17, I awoke to learn of the passing of the Reverend Dr. C. T. Vivian, the legendary civil rights hero who served as a Freedom Rider, was a national director of the Southern Christian Leadership Conference alongside one of its founders, Dr. Martin Luther King Jr., and was an active participant in the 1965 Selma, Alabama, struggle for voting rights. While in Selma, he was infamously assaulted by Sheriff Jim Clark on the Dallas County Courthouse steps. The encounter resulted in a bloody mouth for Dr. Vivian, yet he stood tall and continued to address his oppressors directly. He proclaimed to Clark, "If we are wrong, why don't you arrest us? We were willing to be beaten for democracy, and you misuse democracy in the streets. You beat people bloody in order that they will not have the privilege to vote! You beat me ... then hide your blows."

When I met Dr. Vivian at Ebenezer Baptist Church in Atlanta, I knelt on the ground in reverence before him. I then offered my sincere gratitude for his sacrifices. Our children were present, and I instructed them to tell Dr. Vivian "thank you!"

My youngest child asked, "For what?"

I responded, "For everything."

Before retiring to bed the night that I heard of Dr. Vivian's passing, news broke concerning the death of Congressman John

Lewis. I had the honor of being in the presence of Congressman Lewis on more than one occasion. As I did with Mrs. Rudolph, when in the presence of Congressman Lewis, I studied the scars on his head, evidence of the multiple traumas he experienced while fighting for our freedoms: a crate that came crashing down on him while he was a Freedom Rider in 1961, and the scars left by police batons that also fractured his skull on Selma's Edmund Pettus Bridge in 1965, among many other injuries suffered. As these leaders suddenly became ancestors in the wake of our renewed struggle, it felt as if they were purposely handing over to us a baton and telling us to keep running from here.

On July 30, the final memorial service for Congressman Lewis was held in Atlanta. Earlier that day his final message to the world was published as an essay titled "Together, You Can Redeem the Soul of Our Nation." Lewis wrote,

> Ordinary people with extraordinary vision can redeem the soul of America by getting in what I call good trouble, necessary trouble. Voting and participating in the democratic process are key. The vote is the most powerful nonviolent change agent you have in a democratic society. You must use it because it is not guaranteed. You can lose it.

President Barack Hussein Obama offered a soaring eulogy of Lewis from that hallowed Ebenezer pulpit positioned just above the congressman's flag-draped coffin. Obama called him a "founding father" of a "fuller, fairer, better America." Truer words may never have been spoken. As I viewed both Dr. Vivian and Congressman Lewis' services, my profound sadness was soon replaced with profound gratitude and pride for all that they accomplished for all of us. A month later, on August 28, hundreds of thousands gathered on the Washington Mall in the name of justice, fifty-seven years to the day that the March on Washington for Jobs and Freedom had gathered there. In 1963, John Lewis was the youngest speaker on the platform, and his recent death continued to resonate with those who had gathered anew in 2020.

Though held in a familiar space, the 2020 march felt like the beginning of a new chapter in the pursuit of justice and progress in America. It was at once infuriating and motivating to witness the families victimized by some of the year's most notorious incidents of police violence and white supremacist violence standing boldly together at the very place where Dr. King had once declared, "There are those who are asking the devotees of civil rights, 'When will you be satisfied?' We can never be satisfied as long as the Negro is the victim of the unspeakable horrors of police brutality ... No, no we are not satisfied, and we will not be satisfied until 'justice rolls down like waters and righteousness like a mighty stream.'"[50]

Epilogue

Election Day has always been sacred to me—local, state, federal, it doesn't matter. I rarely miss casting my vote in any election. Always at the forefront of my mind are the tremendous sacrifices that were made to grant me this right and privilege: the blood spilt on the ground, the bones broken, the brutal murders committed in the quest to secure voting rights.

During worship on the Sunday before Election Day in 2020, I was honored to interview Ms. Joanne Bland, the co-founder and former executive director of the National Voting Rights Museum in Selma. I have known Ms. Bland for over fifteen years. She is a frequent speaker on my civil rights pilgrimages. She was present at the Edmund Pettus Bridge on Bloody Sunday, and no matter how many times I hear her tell the story, I shudder when she recalls the sound of a woman's head as it hit the pavement on the bridge when she was knocked down by a mounted Alabama state trooper.

On the first Election Day that I was eligible to vote, I rode my bicycle just over a mile, dressed in a suit and tie despite the humid Houston climate. When I arrived at my polling location, I was completely drenched in sweat, but I was undeterred. I proudly walked in and cast my vote without facing intimidation or molestation. To this day, I dress up to vote in my Sunday best.

I've voted many times since then, but I had never experienced an Election Day like this, and not merely because I was casting my vote in a pandemic. The previous fall, my fiercely independent ninety-two-year-old grandmother, Naomi Forbes Williams, had moved to Dallas to live with my mother. As a coed at Tillotson College (now Huston-Tillotson University) in Austin, Texas, in the early 1940s, she courageously served as president of an interracial student group committed to working toward integration. As a student, she marched with Thurgood Marshall when he served as executive director of the National Association for the Advancement of Colored People's Legal Defense and Educational Fund. Both she and my late grandfather, Bishop W. Williams, were active in their local NAACP branch. They served as poll workers and election judges in Falls County and were frequent delegates to the Texas Democratic Convention. Some of my favorite childhood memories are my summer odysseys with them, meeting such persons as Jesse Jackson Sr. during his second presidential run and Ann Richards during her successful Texas gubernatorial campaign. After forty-four years as an educator, my grandfather retired, only to be elected a county judge, and later a county commissioner. My grandmother, who served thirty-three years as an educator, was right by his side.

Now I had the pleasure of driving my grandmother to the polls to cast her ballot in the historic 2020 election. Although her steps had significantly slowed over the years, her enthusiasm for casting her ballot was not. Any other time, driving my grandmother to the polls for the first time would have been enough to solidify the sacredness of the day, but I had two other very special passengers as well. Beside me sat my amazing wife, Yulise, and inside her womb was our fourth child, a son, whose arrival our entire family was eagerly anticipating the following month. For much of the summer and fall, I had kept a small baby bottle and a bib that read "Black Lives Matter" near our makeshift home production studio, a visual and daily reminder of the lives we are fighting for.

The juxtaposition of it all was almost overwhelming. The moment came with a sense of great responsibility. At once, it was a conversation between my past, my present, and my future, an acknowledgement of the sacrifices of my ancestors and elders. It was a reminder of my responsibility to sacrifice in my own time to secure a better present and future for my children. My grandmother punctuated the special moment by singing a favorite hymn in her sweet soprano voice:

Oh, what a beautiful city
Oh, what a beautiful city
Oh, what a beautiful city
Twelve gates to the city of God

We fulfilled our civic duty and took "vote" stickers for ourselves and our children, born and unborn. We paid a brief, socially distanced visit to members of our church who were providing refreshments outside South Dallas polling locations to encourage voters. Then we took my grandmother back home. Now, all that was left to do was wait for the results of this presidential election between Donald Trump and Joe Biden.

And wait we did, along with the entire nation, shadowed by watchful eyes across the globe. Counting the votes took several days instead of the usual hours, in part because many Republican-led state legislatures had refused to change their archaic laws during a global pandemic to allow counting the exponentially larger number of mail-in ballots before Election Day. The election itself was historic on its face. More Americans cast votes in this presidential election than in any other in the US. Both the winner and loser received more votes than any other presidential candidate in our nation's history. It also soon became apparent that in some states the vote would be decided by only a few thousand ballots.

It was this latter reality that I found most disturbing, but not surprising. Many had hoped that this election would be a clear repudiation of Donald Trump, his administration, and the atrocities enacted in the name of American citizens for four years. Many had hoped that his failure to provide effective national leadership during the pandemic—which unnecessarily resulted in nearly a quarter of a million deaths by Election Day—

would result in a clear rejection of Trumpism. But this did not occur. More white women voted for Donald Trump in 2020 than in 2016. President Trump received his highest-percentage vote counts in American counties experiencing the highest surges of COVID-19. The election appeared to illuminate the truth of President Lyndon Baines Johnson's words on whiteness: "If you can convince the lowest white man he's better than the best colored man, he won't notice you're picking his pocket. Hell, give him somebody to look down on, and he'll empty his pockets for you."[51] To validate Johnson's assertion, no group has been deceived more by President Trump's agenda than poor, uneducated white America.

This election cycle also brought some providential moments. In a tight race in Georgia, voters in the late Congressman John Lewis' district put Biden ahead and delivered Georgia to a Democrat for the first time in nearly thirty years. I could just imagine Lewis doing his "Happy" dance across heaven.

Elsewhere in the nation, millions of Americans proudly voted to reelect a white supremacist president. Former vice president Biden ultimately would emerge the victor. And although Senator Kamala Harris would make history as the first woman, first Black person, first South Asian person, and first person with immigrant parents to be elected vice president of the United States of America—an achievement that brought me great jubilation, in the wake of the election—many began to posture it in a painful context.

Although President Trump's administration was coming to an end, Trumpism was not. Truthfully, Trumpism's roots run deep into the waters of America, just the latest wave of white supremacist and xenophobic hatred that has been present in each American generation.

This is us! The election solidified that something remains in the water. Let's call it hate. Let's call it denying the humanity of all God's creations. Let's call it forsaking the image of God present in every human countenance. Let's call it evil.

Let's call it white supremacy.

On November 7, when Biden was declared the president-elect, Dr. Glaude returned to the air to offer more important wisdom. Although he both understood and encouraged the celebration that the news of Biden's victory had inspired—people dancing in the streets across America and church bells ringing in Paris—he also provided a sobering word.

Glaude said,

> This election is not a referendum. It's a part of the reckoning we're experiencing as a country ... The election revealed to me ... that we are profoundly divided, and those divisions are rooted in some insidious things. We've had four years of Donald Trump. The evidence is clear ... and people still voted for him. In fact, more white people voted for Donald Trump in 2020 than they did in 2016. The reckoning that we're experiencing as a nation ... shows us that race, selfishness, greed, continue to threaten the very life of our Republic and we have to acknowledge that as we move forward.[52]

At the time of this writing, there is no cure for the coronavirus. At the time of this writing, just over a year after a white supremacy-motivated massacre occurred there, there is a mandatory two-week shutdown of all nonessential businesses in El Paso as COVID-19 cases have reached an all-time high. So many people are dying of COVID-19 in El Paso that the morgue is running out of space. Across the nation, COVID-19 cases are skyrocketing, with a new record for new infections nationally being set almost daily.

At present, the best protection that we have against this virus is the care and compassion that we show to one another. It is our intentionality in seeking to not harm one another. It is our willingness to be uncomfortable for a season so that our nation can heal.

To this extent, a virus can heal America. If after many centuries, our collective pain and sorrow can press us toward perfecting our union—a perfection that can be accomplished simply by loving our neighbors as ourselves—and if we embrace our network of mutuality, lay aside our needless divisions, and root out the hate that literally threatens the life of our republic, we can move forward as a nation to become a beloved community.

Yes, there's something in the water. But whether it remains is for each of us to decide.

Notes

[1] W. E. B. DuBois, *The Souls of Black Folk* (New York: Penguin, 1903).

[2] Luke 12:48

[3] Tupac Shakur MTV Interview, 1994, https://www.youtube.com/watch?v=aMXzLhbWtmk.

[4] Psalm 46:4–5

[5] Habakkuk 1:2

[6] 2Pac, Shock G, Eric Baker, Stretch, and Stevie Wonder, "So Many Tears," Interscope, 1995.

[7] Marvin Gaye and James Nyx Jr., "Inner City Blues," Motown Records, 1971.

[8] John Wesley Work II and Frederick J. Work, "Wade in the Water," 1901.

[9] Based on 2 Corinthians 4:7–9

[10] Sam Cooke, "A Change Is Gonna Come," RCA Victor Records, 1964.

[11] Romans 4:17

[12] Martin Luther King Jr., "I've Been to the Mountaintop" address delivered at Mason Temple in Memphis, Tennessee, April 3, 1968.

[13] Amos 5:24

[14] "Get Away, Jordan," A Negro Spiritual, https://www.negrospirituals.com/songs/get_away_jordan.htm.

[15] Amos 5:24

[16] Kate Davidson, "It Would Take 228 Years for Black Families to Amass Wealth of White Families, Analysis Says," *The Wall Street Journal*, April 9, 2016, https://blogs.wsj.com/economics/2016/08/09/it-would-take-228-years-for-black-families-to-amass-wealth-of-white-families-analysis-says/#:~:text=It%20Would%20Take%20228%20Years,Says%20%2D%20Real%20Time%20Economics%20%2D%20WSJ.

[17] Martin Luther King Jr., "Letter from Birmingham Jail," *Why We Can't Wait* (New York: Harper and Row Publishers, 1964).

[18] Martin Luther King Jr., *Where Do We Go from Here: Chaos of Community?* (New York: Harper and Row Publishers, 1967).

[19] Michelle Mark, "Botham Jean's brother gave Amber Guyger a hug after the former cop was sentenced for his brother's murder in a powerful courtroom moment," *Insider*, October 2, 2019, www.insider.com/botham-jeans-brother-forgives-embraces-amber-guyger-2019-10.

[20] Ezekiel 13:10

[21] Martin Luther King Jr., "Remaining Awake Through a Great Revolution" address delivered at the National Cathedral in Washington,

D.C., March 31, 1968, The Martin Luther King, Jr. Research and Education Institute at Stanford University, https://kinginstitute.stanford.edu/king-papers/publications/knock-midnight-inspiration-great-sermons-reverend-martin-luther-king-jr-10.

[22] 1 Corinthians 12:12

[23] Isaiah 54:17; Romans 8:37

[24] Luke 4:18–19

[25] 2 Corinthians 3:17

[26] William Lee, "On 50th anniversary of MLK march in Chicago, a new memorial goes up," The Chicago Tribune, April 4, 2016, https://www.chicagotribune.com/news/ct-mlk-memorial-met-20160805-story.html.

[27] Theresa Walker, "Can We All Just Get Along: Rodney King's Question Still Matters," Orange County Register, April 30, 2017, https://www.mercurynews.com/2017/04/30/can-we-all-just-get-along-rodney-kings-question-still-matters/.

[28] Samuel Osborne, "Black women become most educated group in US," Independent, June 3, 2016, https://www.independent.co.uk/news/world/americas/black-women-become-most-educated-group-us-a7063361.html.

[29] Numbers 13:17–20

[30] Numbers 13:26–33

[31] James Weldon Johnson and J. Rosamond Johnson, "Lift Every Voice and Sing," National Recording Registry, 2016.

[32] Matthew 1:20–23

[33] Luke 4:18–19

[34] Psalm 30:5

[35] "Malcolm X's Fiery Speech Addressing Police Brutality," Smithsonian Magazine, https://www.smithsonianmag.com/videos/category/history/malcolm-xs-fiery-speech-addressing-police-b/.

[36] Sojourner Truth, "Ain't I a Woman?" address delivered at the Women's Rights Convention in Akron, Ohio, May 29, 1851, National Park Service, https://www.nps.gov/articles/sojourner-truth.htm.

[37] Barbara Ransby, Ella Baker and the Black Freedom Movement: A Radical Democratic Vision (Chapel Hill: University of North Carolina Books, 2003).

[38] Adam Kuper and Jessica Kuper, eds, The Social Science Encyclopedia, (London: Routledge, 1989).

[39] W. E. B. DuBois, The Souls of Black Folk (New York: Penguin, 1903).

[40] Martin Luther King Jr., "Letter from Birmingham Jail," Why We Can't Wait (New York: Harper and Row Publishers, 1964).

[41] Marvin Gaye and James Nyx Jr., "Inner City Blues," Motown Records, 1971.

[42] Richard Smallwood, "I Love the Lord," Verity Records, 2006.

[43] James C. Cobb, "When Martin Luther King Jr. Was Killed, He Was Less Popular than Donald Trump Is Today," *USA Today*, April 4, 2018, www.usatoday.com/story/opinion/2018/04/04/martin-luther-king-jr-50-years-assassination-donald-trump-disapproval-column/482242002/.

[44] C. C. J. Carpenter, Joseph A. Durick, Milton L. Grafman, Paul Hardin, Nolan B. Harmon,
George M. Murray, Edward V. Ramage, and Earl Stallings, "Statement by Alabama Clergyman," printed by the American Friends Service Committee, April 12, 1963, The Martin Luther King, Jr. Research and Education Institute at Stanford University, https://kinginstitute.stanford.edu/sites/mlk/files/lesson-activities/clergybirmingham1963.pdf.

[45] Exodus 1:9–10, *New Living Translation*

[46] Exodus 1:11–14, *New Living Translation*

[47] Exodus 12:21–23, *New Living Translation*

[48] Hebrews 12:1, *New Living Translation*

[49] John Henrik Clarke as quoted in Derrick Young, "Quick Review: Christopher Columbus and the Afrikan Holocaust," Mahogany Books, April 3, 2017, https://blackbooksmatter.com/quick-review-christopher-columbus-and-the-afrikan-holocaust/.

[50] Martin Luther King, Jr., "I Have a Dream" address delivered at the March on Washington for Jobs and Freedom, August 28, 1968, The Martin Luther King, Jr. Research and Education Institute at Stanford University, https://kinginstitute.stanford.edu/king-papers/documents/i-have-dream-address-delivered-march-washington-jobs-and-freedom

[51] Bill D. Moyers, "What a Real President Was Like," *The Washington Post* , November 31, 1988, www.washingtonpost.com/archive/opinions/1988/11/13/what-a-real-president-was-like/d483c1be-d0da-43b7-bde6-04e10106ff6c/.

[52] Eddie Glaude, "Eddie Glaude on the Nation's Reckoning with the Presidential Election," *Morning Joe*, MSNBC, November 7, 2020, https://www.facebook.com/273864989376427/videos/1013760549196159.